BLEED, BLISTER, PUKE, AND PURGE

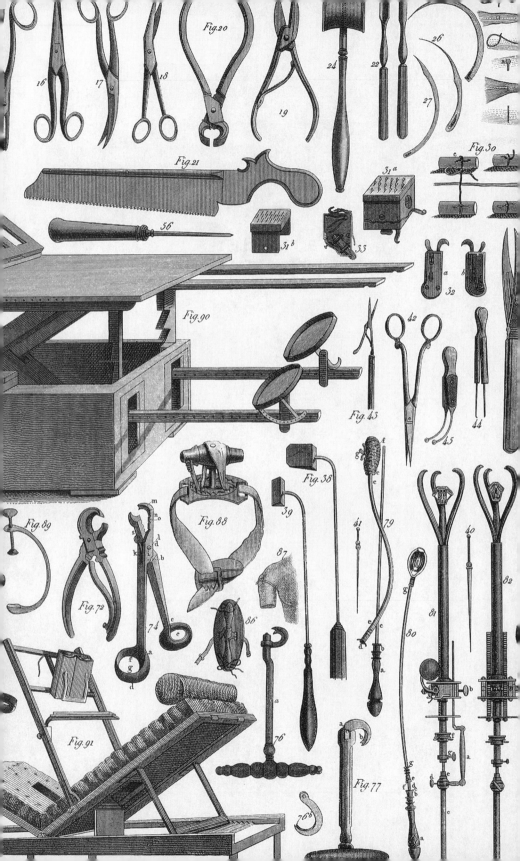

BLEED, BLISTER, PUKE, AND PURGE

THE DIRTY SECRETS BEHIND EARLY AMERICAN MEDICINE

J. MARIN YOUNKER

ZEST BOOKS

TABLE OF CONTENTS

To Sameer: Contrary to popular belief, middle age is pretty damn awesome and it all started with you.

ZEST BOOKS

- zestbooks.net/blog
- zestbooks.tumblr.com

- twitter.com/zestbooks
- facebook.com/BooksWithATwist

2443 Fillmore Street, Suite 340, San Francisco, CA 94115 | www.zestbooks.net

Part III
Anesthesia and Civil War Medicine

Part IV
The Death of Heroic Medicine

Part I
MEDICINE IN THE NEW OLD WORLD

Chapter 1
A DIRTY BUSINESS

In 1862, during the Battle of Fredericksburg, Union soldier Corporal Quick was shot behind the jaw—and survived. It took five days for him to be admitted to a hospital because treating wounded soldiers wasn't a military priority. By the time Quick reached the hospital, the left side of his face was severely bruised, and his left eye was swollen shut. The doctors prescribed bed rest and the washing of his face, and also recommended—well, there's no other way to say it—pooping. However, after a week of this "treatment," Quick began bleeding profusely from his mouth and nose. The doctors shoved a wad of dirty cloth up his nose to staunch the flow, but when that didn't work they were forced to their last resort: They tied off a major artery in his neck. Quick was awake for the entire procedure.

What the doctors didn't realize is that this artery, now known as the common carotid, supplies most of the blood to the head, neck, and brain. For days after the surgery, Quick was delirious and unable to swallow any food or drink. Nine days later, he finally died in a pool of his own diarrhea, with a severely infected incision that leaked pus and blood. If the bullet had hit his brain, it is very unlikely he would have suffered anywhere near as much as he eventually did.

For most of its history—until well into the twentieth century, in fact—American medicine has been a foul and dirty business. Unlike the rigorous medical education of today, there was no formal schooling, no exams to measure competency, no way to practice and learn from experience without causing harm, and no professional rules or regulations. Instead, the typical therapy was to "bleed, blister, puke, and purge." More often than not, the patient suffered and died at the hands of well-intentioned but undereducated physicians who simply didn't know any better, and the ones who did survive attributed the cures to superstition, miracles, or completely inappropriate methods. There was little to no connection between science and medicine; entire populations were wiped out from plagues, many women died in childbirth, many children didn't make it to adulthood, and the average life expectancy was shockingly low. That's not to say that doctors failed to learn anything from their work. But generally speaking, discoveries in the field translated into very little progress, as they were either ignored or misapplied to traditional therapies. There was, in other words, no escape from the barbarism. Rich and poor, famous and unknown, young and old, all suffered alike.

So how did today's sophisticated medicine—one of face transplants and DNA mapping—come from such crude beginnings? To answer that question, we'll need to take a trip back in time, to when Europeans first arrived in what they termed "the New World". . . ●

Chapter 2
THE EARLY ROOTS

Arriving in the New World

In a nutshell, colonists came to America for either religious freedom or profit. But once there, things weren't easy. The Roanoke colonists (1585) didn't survive at all, disappearing after just five years in the New World. But in 1607, with the help of local Native Americans who gave them food, water, and agricultural advice, desperate Jamestown settlers succeeded where their predecessors had failed. George Percy, who served as the governor of Jamestown, described the grim early months of Jamestown:

> Our men were destroyed with cruel diseases, as Swellings, Fluxes, Burning Fevers, and by wars, and some departed suddenly, but for the most part they died of mere famine. . . . Our food was but a small Can of Barley sod in water, to five men a day, our drink cold water taken out of the River, which was at a flood very salty, at a low tide full of slime and filth, which was the destruction of many of our men. Thus we lived for the space of five months in this miserable distress, not having five able men to man our Bulwarks upon any occasion.

If it had not pleased God to have put a terror in the Savages'[1] hearts, we had all perished by those wild and cruel Pagans, being in that weak estate as we were; our men night and day groaning in every corner of the Fort most pitiful to hear.

Without help from the Powhatans, the uniformly male Jamestown colonists—who were city-dwellers, not farmers—would most likely have gone the way of the Lost Colony of Roanoke. Still, in the first six months, 51 of the 120 colonists died of illness or famine. Settlers resorted to eating their horses, dogs, rats, leather shoes, belts—and even each other.

Ultimately, reestablished trade with the Native Americans, additional mission supplies, and the arrival of women secured Jamestown's future until the early 1700s. Also aided by Native American goodwill, the Puritan families of *Mayflower* fame (1620) were more immediately successful in their settlement, avoiding the extreme distress endured by Jamestown's colonists. Though unprepared for the harsh New England winter, low on supplies, and battling disease, the Puritan settlers benefited greatly from their superior farming skills. The original Plymouth colony was absorbed into the greater Massachusetts Bay Colony in 1691.

Adapting European Ways

Immigrants did their best to replicate the Old World in the New, yet the more strictly organized European medical system did not make the crossing to America. In Europe, there were generally three types of professionals who offered medical care: physicians, surgeons, and apothecaries. Physicians had at least a formal education, and as a result, were the most highly regarded. Surgeons were more along the lines of tradesmen, learning mostly through apprenticeships. And apothecaries were similar to modern pharmacists in that they were largely responsible for mixing drugs (though they were on par with surgeons as far as reputation and education were concerned).

---

1. "Savages" is the derogatory word used by Europeans for indigenous populations, a commentary on their racist belief that their white society's practices were more "civilized."

Duck, Duck, Goose

Unfortunately, the general lack of both medical knowledge and medical professionals left plenty of room for quacks to make a quick profit. The term "quack" (used to describe an unscrupulous doctor, eager to turn a profit on less-than-helpful remedies) is derived from the Dutch word *quacksalver*, a reference to the mercury added to creams by European physicians who were unintentionally—and ironically—poisoning their patients. Benjamin Franklin himself said, "Quacks are the greatest liars in the world except their patients."

In America, without the prestigious university medical training available, colonial physicians learned primarily through apprenticeships. All apprenticeships were not created equal, varying greatly in quality. It was not uncommon for a medical student to embark on his career without having seen a skeleton or an anatomical chart of the body. Apprenticeship duties as assigned included anything from the impractical—caring for the physician's horse and keeping the shop's fire going—to the more useful tasks of mixing drugs and shadowing patient visits.

Because physicians were expensive and surgeons were rare, colonists were less concerned about the division between physicians and surgeons, and also turned to a minister–physician for medical attention. This was only natural since the clergy were trusted, educated, and could address any spiritual concerns that might be plaguing a patient worried about meeting his maker. (It was also convenient to have a religious figure on hand to play the role of both physician *and* minister in the probable likelihood of death.)

During the colonial era, the medical profession didn't pay enough to support even one person, let alone a whole family, so most colonial physicians held multiple jobs. One famous physician of the time advised medical students to leave the cities and start rural medical practices instead—that way they could also farm for extra income. Because colonists often couldn't afford medical care, goods (rather than coins) were typical forms of payment: a pig in exchange for setting a broken bone, or pears for reducing a fever.

Herbal Cures

Practically speaking, people at the time usually relied on apothecaries or druggists for treatment—which meant a lot of herbal and natural remedies. Native American healers, who had hundreds of years of experience using local plants, played an important role in early American herbal medicine. A cure for malaria (quinine), a remedy for heart irregularities (foxglove), and a precursor to modern aspirin (willow bark) all originate from Native American herbal therapies. The tribal shaman, or healer, occupied a role as both a physical and spiritual healer, prescribing herbs and activities to restore harmony between the physical and spiritual worlds. Some of those healers passed their knowledge of the local flora and fauna on to early settlers. Lame Deer (1903-1976), a Sioux holy man, explained why "medicine man" was not an accurate description of his role: "That's a white man's word like squaw, papoose, Sioux, tomahawk–words that don't exist in the Indian language. I wish there were better words to make clear what 'medicine man' stands for, but I can't." Native American herbal knowledge was, however, futile against the killers of the Old World—smallpox, measles, and yellow fever. Millions of native people died from these imported diseases, some given to them deliberately, with entire cultural groups on the verge of extinction.

Given the suspect medical practices of the time, any actual healing with herbal and natural remedies was most likely due to luck rather than real expertise. Herbal medicine depended on plants whose potency was neither reliable nor regulated, making it a very inexact science. As American medical historian William G. Rothstein said, ". . . the same prescription compounded by ten different physicians or pharmacists (physicians usually compounded their own drugs during this period) would probably look, taste, and act differently in each instance." Forget quality control.

Superstitions Instead of Science

Medicine without science meant that superstitions masqueraded as medical remedies in early America. Here's just one example: Colonists believed that warts were cured by either applying water collected from a rotting tree stump, rubbing the offending wart

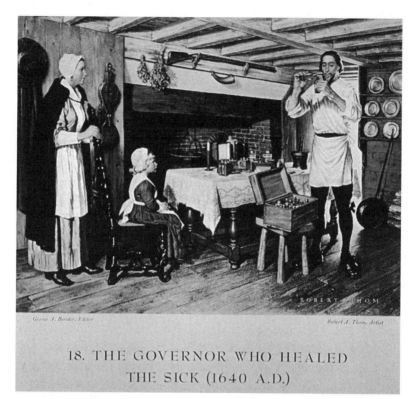

18. THE GOVERNOR WHO HEALED THE SICK (1640 A.D.)

George A. Bender, Editor

Robert A. Thom, Artist

with raw potato slices or meat, or holding one's hands up in the air during an expanding moon. They also believed that dried and powdered toads could be used as a cure for the super-contagious smallpox virus (and, uh, it didn't work). Birthmarks were rubbed with the hand of a corpse in attempts to remove them. A supposed remedy for chickenpox was to lie down in a chicken coop after sunset and let a black hen fly over you. A spider-laced syrup was used to treat a fever. To restore sight to the blind, the eyes of an owl were placed on the affected eyelids. And best of all, one treatment for head lice instructed sufferers to wash their head with whiskey and sand; in turn, the lice were supposed to get drunk and fight each other to the death.

Legitimate and effective cures were hard to come by, and a physician's treatment likely wouldn't perform much better than doing nothing at all—and often did worse!

A description of medical advice from a London expert to John Winthrop, the first governor of the Massachusetts Bay Colony and acting physician for the area, gives some clue about the level of care for the time:

> For soare brests, take yolkes of eggs and honie alike, beat them till they be very thinn; then with wheat flower beat them, till it be as thick as hony: spread it upon flax, and lay it upon the breast, defending the nipple with a plate of leas as bigg as an halfe crowne, and a hole in it so begg that ye nipple may come out—renewe it every twelve hours: and this will breake and coole the brest.

From the above description, the ailment is unclear ("sore breasts" are a symptom of many separate maladies), and there is no explanation for why honey, eggs, and flax—ingredients usually combined to make bread—would be helpful in this cause.

Without germ theory, physicians didn't understand the causes of illnesses, thus reducing symptoms was the name of the game. Any positive change in the symptoms, even if only briefly, was considered a success. The physician William Douglass (1691-1752) admitted of the time:

> In general the physical practice in our colonies is so perniciously bad that, excepting in surgery and some very acute cases, it is better to let nature, under a proper regimen, take her course than to trust to the honesty and sagacity of the practitioner. . . Frequently there is more danger from the physician than from the distemper.

It's a wonder any colonists survived.

Two Medical Greats

To avoid the impression that Western medicine was completely useless, it's worth taking a moment to recognize a couple of influential figures. Giovanni Batista Morgagni (1682–1771), for instance, kept meticulous patient records and dissected human bodies to further his education. Dissection helped Morgagni determine that diseases and death were tied directly to a specific organ or part of the body, which was a major departure and improvement from previous medical theories that supposed internal and external imbalances were the cause of death. In 1761, Morgagni published five books that recorded 700 patient case histories with an extensive index. Those cases represented fifty-five years of work. Reflecting on his life, Morgagni observed, "I have passed my life amidst books and cadavers."

John Hunter (1728–1793) offers another example of knowledge in the midst of ignorance. Hunter was a renowned Scottish surgeon who contributed real research and factual knowledge to medicine through his scientific approach to surgery. His day-to-day observations filled ten volumes of handwritten notes that recorded and spread his novel ideas. Like Morgagni, Hunter also focused on human dissection, and he built an extensive collection of medical specimens that would one day lead to one of the greatest anatomical museums in the world: London's Hunterian Museum. Hunter's anatomical and pathological museum, and others like it, was an important teaching tool for a profession that was in dire need of one. ❋

No Glove, No Love

There is a well-known medical urban legend about John Hunter auto-experimenting, i.e., trying out medical procedures on himself, which might or might not be an urban legend. At the time, physicians couldn't tell apart the various sexually transmitted diseases, relying only on symptoms (which were often hard to tell apart) for diagnoses. Legend goes that Hunter was so zealous in his research on STDs that he went to a local pub and found a sailor with a case of first-stage syphilis, scraped the ooze from the man's penis, and transferred it to his own. (Don't try this at home.) Unknowingly to Hunter, his sailor had both syphilis *and* gonorrhea, which complicated and confused things significantly (and probably didn't make Hunter's life any easier either). Hunter published his findings,

CONTINUED ON NEXT PAGE ...

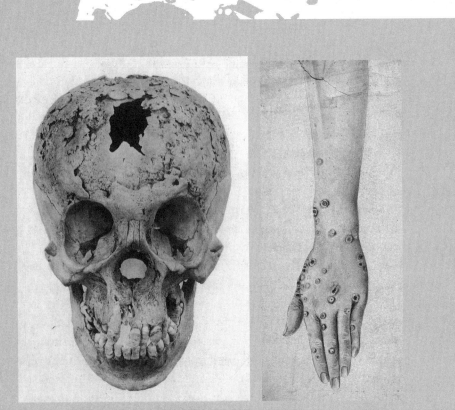

SYPHILIS OF SKULL AND ARM, COURTESY OF WIKICOMMONS

which helped to perpetuate the myth that syphilis and gonorrhea were the same disease—a myth which persisted for another seventy years. Even the greats made mistakes.

Syphilis is a sexually transmitted disease that was difficult to detect, and its origins are still under debate. Around the time of Christopher Columbus, an epidemic of syphilis occurred in Italy. Did Columbus and his sailors bring the disease back from the New World, or did the STD already exist in Europe before 1494? Forensic anthropology suggests that it was most likely a disease they picked up in the Americas, but either way, without the widespread use of condoms, syphilis spread. Although there are references to condom-like devices in Egypt, Greece, and other ancient civilizations, cheap, mass-produced condoms weren't commonly available until the mid-1800s. (Goodyear, the tire company, started mass-producing rubber condoms in 1855.)

Early syphilis treatments included poking the sores with hot irons, "sitting in sulphur baths, and swallowing an assortment of medicines and boiled ant nests. . . ." All were throwbacks to the torturous prescriptions of the sixteenth century. It wasn't until 1838 that syphilis was differentiated from gonorrhea, and the three stages of syphilis were identified. (Fair warning: this is not going to be pretty.) In the first stage, a painless sore develops at the point of contact. And since transmission occurs sexually, that tended to mean the genitals. By the second stage, the infected person breaks out in a rash and experiences flu-like symptoms. And last but not least, the third (or "tertiary") stage is mostly internal: The bacteria, having spread throughout the body, eat their way through the skull and organs while the person is still alive. The duration of each stage can last anywhere from weeks to years, and an effective cure (in the form of salvarsan, an arsenic-based drug), wasn't discovered until the early 1900s. Ultimately, in 1943, penicillin was discovered as the cure for syphilis.

A German knight, Ulrich von Hutten (1488-1523), recorded his observations of (and personal experience with) syphilis in the early sixteenth century:

> From the boils there emitted a foul, dark green pus. This secretion was so vile that even the burning pains of the boils troubled the sick less than their horror at the sight of their own bodies. Yet this was only the beginning. People's flesh and skin filled with water; their bladders developed sores; their stomachs were eaten away.
>
> The symptoms progressively got worse: the syphilis pustules developed into ulcers that dissolved skin, muscle, bone, palate, and tonsils — even lips, noses, eyes, and genital organs. Rubbery tumors, filled with white, sticky mucus, grew to the size of rolls of bread. And many of the people died.

An accurate and horrifying description and a reminder to be thankful for modern medicine.

Chapter 3
ON DISPLAY

Not all colonial Americans relied on superstitions, however. Some went to Europe for their medical education and set out to instruct future practitioners with lectures featuring human specimens and models, which were invaluable. The below is an advertisement for Philadelphian physician Dr. Chovet's (1704-1790) medical lectures, which included exceptional preserved and wax body parts:

> At the anatomical museum in Videl's alley, Second Street, on Wednesday, the seventh of December, at six in the evening, Dr. Chovet will begin his course of Anatomical and Physiological lectures, in which the several parts of the human body will be demonstrated, with their mechanism and actions, together with the doctrines of life, health, and the several effects resulting from the actions of the parts; on his curious collection of anatomical wax-works, and other natural preparations; to be continued the whole winter until the course is completed. As this course cannot be attended with the disagreeable sight or smell of recent deceased and putrid carcases, which often disgust even the students of Physic, as well as the curious, otherwise inclined to this useful and sublime part of natural philosophy, it is hoped this undertaking will meet with suitable encouragement.

Keep it Clean

Chovet was known for his sarcasm and eccentricities. During a downpour, Chovet borrowed a coat from a Quaker who simply asked the physician to avoid swearing while wearing it. (Also known as the Religious Group of Friends, Quakers are Christians who subscribe to, among many other things, an honest life without swearing, especially blaspheming.) When returning the coat, the Quaker asked Chovet if had managed to honor the agreement, and Chovet replied: "No, but there was a damnable disposition to lie." Double whammy.

A strong stomach was obviously required. Advertising the touchable and movable medical specimens was the mark of a superior lecture, as it was not common for medical courses to include anything other than a talking head and, possibly, a two-dimensional textbook.

Cabinets of Curiosity

The idea for Dr. Chovet's collection, as well as Hunter's, was born out of cabinets of curiosity. As a show of worldliness and money, the wealthy and the noble often took the time to collect and display unusual objects from around the world in a room called a *wunderkammer* (German for "wonder room"). The first record of a cabinet of curiosity is from 1599. That original cabinet was owned by an Italian apothecary, and included a stuffed crocodile that hung from its ceiling (which later became a staple of the genre). These (usually private) cabinets and rooms included everything from animal and human skeletons to art, taxidermied animals, mummies, books, and sometimes even renderings of mythical creatures (unicorns' skeletons could be cobbled together with horse bones and a narwhal's tusk, for instance). The more unique the specimens, the better.

Sometimes, collectors even included live exhibits of "abnormal" humans. In 1718, Tsar Peter the Great (1672–1725) issued an edict for his new St. Petersburg museum, seeking monsters, both human and animal, living and dead. Peter deemed a young boy, Foma, a worthy-enough "monster" for display. In fact, Foma only had a deformity of his hands and feet: He had just two fingers on each hand

and two toes on each foot. Nevertheless, when Foma died young, Peter the Great had him stuffed like a piece of furniture.

Given the foreign origins and exotic nature of its objects, a wunderkammer required a great deal of money to build. Some curators used their collections to further their popularity among the elite; others thought it showed off their smarts. It wasn't uncommon for a collector to become obsessed with a specific item. One overzealous curator amassed more than one hundred bird and animal eggs.

By the 1800s, the popularity of wunderkammers waned, and many of the collections were sold off to become part of specialized or public museums.

Shocking the Public with Freak Shows

It didn't take long for an outrageous version of the wunderkammer to pop up for the masses. In England and America, during the Victorian era (1837–1901), "freak shows" and museums—light on science but heavy on the bizarre—were major attractions. Some public museums were open to men only, as they were considered inappropriate for women and children. These exhibitions included giants, bearded ladies, dwarves, tattooed indigenous people, and conjoined twins. One of the most famous of these was owned by P.T. Barnum (of Barnum & Bailey Circus fame). He purchased slave Joice Heth for exhibit. The aged, blind, and partially paralyzed African American Heth was advertised as being 161 years old and a former nurse to George Washington. Barnum envisioned Heth giving sage advice to his paying customers. At one point, during Heth's waning popularity, Barnum anonymously claimed in a newspaper letter that Heth was a robot. When Heth died, Barnum hired a physician to publicly dissect Heth, charging the audience money. Barnum's reprehensible treatment of Heth is emblematic of the attitudes that dehumanized and commoditized Africans and African Americans.

In 1841, Barnum opened his Barnum American Museum in New York City and filled it with exhibits and curios, many of which were outright frauds and hoaxes. One of his most famous exhibits, that of the Feejee or Fiji Mermaid (a reference to its "exotic" origins from the faraway South Pacific), was falsely legitimized by a "doctor" who lectured on the topic of mermaids. "Dr. J. Griffin" was, in fact, a friend of Barnum's who used a fake mustache and British accent as part of his disguise, and the "mermaid" in question was actually just the upper body of a monkey attached to the lower body of a fish—a creation which owes its roots to Japanese folklore. (Shown in historical drawings, Japanese mermen, known as *ningyo*, were more ferocious versions of their Western mythological counterparts, which were typically depicted the naked torso of a beautiful woman.)

Barnum capitalized on the public's deep scientific curiosity and its desire to learn more about the world beyond its immediate surroundings. The masses delighted in the wonder and mystery of Barnum's exhibits. A true showman with an impeccable sense of timing, Barnum would pull a fraudulent exhibit before protests could erupt. He thus became known as the "Prince of Humbugs." Ultimately, Barnum was a man of his time. Members of the public went along with his antics for the most part, implying that they felt that they were at least getting their money's worth.

Medical Collections for Physicians

Anatomical and pathological museums were nothing like the titillating freak shows peddled by Barnum and his competitors. In the eighteenth and nineteenth centuries, some cabinets evolved into specialized collections created by learned men intent on learning more about their respective fields. This was a departure from the wunderkammer's broad, and often eclectic, inventory of oddities and wonders. These teaching collections were often later incorporated into medical colleges, educating aspiring doctors and experienced physicians alike. They were not open to the public.

Skeletons, specimens, medical instruments, books, and anatomical replicas were essential to these medical collections. Lifelike wax models were crafted to look like body parts, both healthy and diseased. Since there was limited access to cadavers, wax models were more helpful to an inexperienced physician than simply looking at a textbook's flat drawing or hearing secondhand knowledge from a professor. Plus, wax didn't rot or smell, and didn't need to be replaced every few days. (Plaster was used for the same reason.)

Wax replicas of the human form have a long and even distinguished history, from death masks to complete figures in the Marie

Wax On, Wax Off

One of the most dramatic wax models is that of Madame Dimanche, a French woman who suffered from a horn-like tumor protruding from her forehead. An 1851 report indicates that by the time Madame Dimanche's horn was removed by a surgeon—six years after it was first noticed—the growth was almost 10 inches long and was so heavy that Dimanche held it up with a sack that she attached to her nightcap. This begs the question: Why did she wait so long? Madame Dimanche finally relented to surgery at the advanced age of eighty-two because, by that point, she had become worried about meeting her maker with a so-called satanic ornament attached to her skull. The surgeon removed the horn at the base, along with the skin to which it was attached. This was Dimanche's third tumor; she had previously removed a tumor from her cheek by herself, while a different surgeon cut another from her thumb.

Tussaud (1761–1850) style. The medical application of wax became prevalent in Europe shortly after the Renaissance. Artists of the time would work closely with the anatomist or surgeon to produce life-like re-creations, which often had removable parts that revealed the body's inner layers, like the intestines or a fetus. The graphic wax models remain both beautiful and disturbing today.

Two well-known European modelers were Joseph Towne (1806–1879) and Jules Pierre Francois Baretta (1834–1923). Towne concentrated much of his work during the mid-to-late 1800s on the study of dermatology and skin diseases, producing more than 550 wax models. Parisian artist Baretta began his work with papier-mâché fruit, moving on to wax models in 1865. At the time of his death, Baretta had created more than two thousand wax models. Like Towne's, Baretta's models were mostly of skin diseases, which were better represented by the realistic, 3-D wax models than by other media. However, both Towne and Baretta refused to reveal their trade secrets to others, so their methods of working with wax died with them.

True-to-life replicas and preserved specimens allowed inexperienced physicians to see typical and unusual examples of diseases and conditions, but medical education still had a ways to go. ✹

Chapter 4
TAKING CARE

The First Hospital

Anatomical models and specimens did much to enrich the educational experiences available to budding physicians and surgeons. Today's doctors also benefit from residencies at hospitals where years of intense, hands-on experience supplements their classroom learning. Hospitals are a relatively modern creation, but once they arrived on the scene they proved quite important for improving the overall state of medical education. Hospitals originally served as guesthouses that provided food, clothing, and shelter; they didn't have any real medical purpose at all until the eighteenth century. Seeking to copy British hospitals that treated the poor, Dr. Thomas Bond opened America's first hospital in Philadelphia in 1752, and moved it to its current location in 1756. Pennsylvania Hospital was the first step in establishing Philadelphia as the birthplace of American medicine. Founders intended to help those who couldn't afford medical care and to provide for the city's mentally ill—who were not only vulnerable to being prayed upon, but were sometimes a danger to themselves and others. The founders outlined their wishes in the petition to open the Pennsylvania Hospital, read to the House of Representatives of the Province of Pennsylvania in January 1751:

> *To the honourable House of Representatives of the Province of Pennsylvania*
>
> The petition of sundry inhabitants of the Provence,
> HUMBLY SHOWETH

That with the numbers of people the numbers of lunaticks, or persons distempered in mind, and deprived of their rational faculties, hath greatly increased in this province.

That some of them going at large, are a terrour to their neighbors, who are daily apprehensive of the violences they may commit; and others are continually wasting their substance, to the great injury of themselves and families, ill disposed persons wickedly taking advantage of their unhappy condition, and drawing them into unreasonable bargains, &c. . . .

Your petitioners beg leave to further represent, that though the good laws of this province have made many compassionate and charitable provisions for the relief of the poor, yet something farther seems wanting in favour of such whose poverty is made more miserable by the weight of a grievous disease, from which they might be easily relieved. . . .

The above reasons didn't immediately rally potential supporters, however, and Bond quickly realized his friend Benjamin Franklin's influence would be essential. It pays to have friends in high places, after all. With Franklin's support, frugal politicians agreed to match contributions raised by the hospital's fundraisers. Franklin said of his efforts: "I do not remember any of my political maneuvers, the success of which gave me at the time more pleasure."

Initially, two of the six physicians hired at the hospital agreed to work for free for a year. Bond, the third physician, took it one step

Nice Specimens

Upon viewing Chovet's collection, John Adams said it was one of the ". . . most admirable, exquisite representations of the whole animal economy. Four complete skeletons, a leg with all the nerves, veins, and arteries injected with wax, two complete bodies in wax, full grown; waxen representations of all the muscles, tendons, &c., of the head, brain, heart, lungs, liver, stomach, &c." Quality medical specimens impressed everyone.

More Blood and Gore, Please

An observer once said of a surgery by Dr. Bond,

> I had the curiosity last week to be present at the hospital, at Dr. Bond's cutting for stone, and was agreeably disappointed, for instead of seeing an operation, said to be perplexed with difficulty and uncertainty, and attended with violence and cruelty, it was performed with such ease, regularity, and success, that it scarcely gave a shock to the most sympathizing bystander, the whole being completed, and a stone of two inches in length, and one in diameter, extracted in less than two minutes.

Bond was known for his exceptional surgical skill and speed in removing kidney and bladder stones.

further and signed on to work his first *three* years without pay. Pennsylvania Hospital's budget included enough money to treat up to seventy patients at a time at no charge. Those with the ability to pay, however, were charged a small fee, and slave owners were charged more for the care of their slaves. (Some speculate that it may have been an attempt by the abolitionist Quaker managers to exact punishment on the slave owners.)

Another source for the hospital's income was its medical library. In 1762, a Dr. Fothergill gifted anatomical drawings and casts to the organization. These specimens were added to an already on-hand human skeleton, which formed the beginnings of the hospital's anatomical collection and library—the first of its kind in the country. Because of the collection's educational value, a small fee was charged for related lectures, which boosted the organization's bank account.

As Fothergill noted, the drawings and casts were especially useful in an environment where cadavers for dissection were scarce. Dr. Chovet's wax models were later added to this educational bounty, providing lifelike medical reproductions for study. Pennsylvania Hospital's collection and others like it were a real treasure.

Proof against Prejudice

Pervasive societal prejudices meant that educated men—physicians included—sought scientific proof for the racial and ethnic superiority of Europeans, which didn't do much for equality. Skulls were of particular importance to scientists who believed that God made whites superior to all other races and ethnicities. Some physical anthropologists of the time also studied human remains, specifically the cranial size, to prove the superiority of whites over blacks.

Two skull collections in Philadelphia, Joseph Hyrtl's and Samuel G. Morton's, provide particular insight into the debate over ethnic supremacy, especially as it related to phrenology—or the study of the human skull, which peaked in popularity from the 1820s through the 1840s. This pseudoscience claimed that there were twenty-seven distinct areas of the brain, each with a specific function or ability, like kindness, or the ability to see colors. The size and shape of a particular section would theoretically determine a person's ability or strength.

A Viennese surgeon and professor, Joseph Hyrtl (1810-1894), delighted in collecting all kinds of specimens, including more than eight hundred types of fish and human skulls. Part of Hyrtl's collection—139 skulls in total—eventually made its way to the Mütter Museum. These skulls were supposed to illustrate the physical differences among ethnic and cultural groups in Eastern Europe. Some of the skulls were obtained through nefarious means, such as grave robbing.

Written on most of the skulls are the person's name, age, birthplace, religion, employment, and cause of death. Only fourteen of the skulls are from women, one of which belonged to

PHRENOLOGY CHART, COURTESY OF THE NATIONAL LIBRARY OF MEDICINE

a well-known prostitute in Vienna who died of meningitis at the age of nineteen. Some of the stories read quite dramatically: suicide after a failed affair and blood loss after a cult member cut off his own testicles.

Also fascinated with crania, Philadelphian Samuel G. Morton (1799-1851), a doctor and a leader in physical anthropology, amassed 867 skulls. Morton believed that God had established the different races after the Great Flood so that each would have the ability to thrive in its own particular environment. With his cranial collection, Morton sought to prove that white people had bigger skulls, and that bigger skulls meant bigger brains, which meant more smarts—with Caucasians at the top and Africans at the bottom. In Morton's view, this justified slavery. Morton was not alone in his flawed and insulting conclusion.

DR. HYRTL AND A SKULL, COURTESY OF THE NATIONAL LIBRARY OF MEDICINE

Hyrtl strongly disagreed with Morton's hierarchy of races in which Caucasians were taken to be innately superior in matters of intellect. On the contrary, Hyrtl believed his skulls showed that the physical measurements of a skull did not directly relate to intelligence—that bigger wasn't necessarily better. It was his collection of skulls, all from the same geographic area and all Caucasian, which made his case. Unfortunately, this evidence didn't have widespread influence, and debate raged for more than a century. Of course, we now know that skull size has no impact on intelligence.

Treatment for Almost All

Much of the motivation for creating the hospital was financial. In 1750, Philadelphia was the most populous colonial city, with more than 15,000 people—many of them poor and looking to cash in on the city's opportunities. When lots of people are crowded into housing with unsanitary conditions, it can often lead to disease. Treating the poor at the hospital saved on public expense, since it was cheaper to treat them in the hospital than at home. Physician house calls were the luxury of the rich. Whereas, if hospital staff could cure a poor man, neither he nor his family would become a burden on society. Everybody won—at least in theory.

People from all walks of life received care, and not just the wealthy and those of European descent. The hospital treated Native Americans and slaves alongside property-holding whites. Physicians, however, were not without prejudice: Race, social position, and gender didn't go unnoticed. For the first half of the 1800s, blacks received segregated care. Women with young children were not allowed to be patients unless the children were cared for off-site. And unmarried pregnant women were denied care in order to avoid sending the message that the hospital accepted their supposed "lives of sin." However, men who impregnated said sinful women were not held to the same standard. Like slave owners, patients suffering from venereal diseases were also charged an extra fee for their immoral behavior.

Others not allowed at Pennsylvania Hospital included those without hope for a cure (*except* in the case of mental afflictions) and those with smallpox or a contagious disease characterized by fever or cough. Once isolated facilities were built to allow for quarantine, people with infectious diseases were given treatment. ✦

Chapter 5

INSANE IN THE MEMBRANE

When Pennsylvania Hospital first opened its doors, four of the first six patients admitted suffered from mental illnesses of various kinds. It didn't hurt that treating the insane was a financial boon (the wealthy could afford to send a mentally ill relative to outside care for treatment and didn't hesitate to do so, alleviating their households of the personal burden). Most were informally admitted to the hospital, often with a scrap of paper attesting to lunacy with the promise to pay for the patient's board and funeral expenses in the event of death. If the attending physician committed the patient, there was no process of appeal for the patient.

It's doubtful that those treated for mental illness would've agreed with the sentiment expressed by Francis Scott Key, the author of *The Star Spangled Banner*, who wrote in 1857,

"On Visiting the Pennsylvania Hospital"

Whose fair abode is this? Whose happy lot
Has drawn them in these peaceful shades to rest,
And hear the distant hum of busy life?
The city's noise, its clouds of smoke and dust,
Vainly invade these leafy walls that wave
On high around it, sheltering all within,
And wooing the scared bird to stay its flight

And add its note of joy to bless the scene:
The city's toils, and cares, and strifes are, sure,
Alike excluded here—Content here smiles
And reigns, and leads her vot'ries through the maze
Of flower-embroidered walks to bowers of bliss:
O! 'tis a sight to warm the heart of him
Who feels for man, and shares the joys he sees.

This poem paints a pretty scene that is woefully at odds with the actual standard of care for the mentally ill at Pennsylvania Hospital.

Mistreating the Mentally Ill

Historically, treatment was not kind to the mentally ill. During the Middle Ages, people with mental illnesses were thought to suffer from demonic possession or witchcraft. Supposedly, a full moon was particularly detrimental on one's sanity, hence the term *lunacy,* which comes from *luna,* the Latin word for moon. Other than the work of the devil and the moon's influence, other causes for diseases of the mind were erroneously attributed to, among other things, a broken heart or religious visions. These falsehoods persisted until the early nineteenth century. "Madness" or "melancholy" were generic terms labeling a patient's behavior. Based on this information, historic labels of "insane" or "lunatic" are dubious at best—without modern science, one cannot be sure of the true nature of the mental illness or if there was one at all, as epilepsy was identified early on as demonic possession. (To be sure, modern medicine still does not completely understand the causes of and treatments for mental illnesses.)

Those regarded as mad were sometimes stoned, tormented, or removed from their homes and sent to live elsewhere. Psychiatry as a study didn't come into being until the late 1700s and wasn't identified as a specific branch of study until 1808 in Germany. With the emergence of psychiatry, reforms were first made in European madhouses to put an end to the outright cruelty inflicted on the mentally afflicted. This was especially true in England with the very public treatment of mad King George III, who some speculate suffered from a metabolic disease or who may have been a manic-depressive. A "mad" king humanized mental illness and generated

Straighten Up

In 1790, a French upholsterer came up with a way of subduing out-of-control patients that was, in its way, an improvement on previous methods. Instead of relying on ropes and chains, he devised a jacket with overly long arms, fitted like a coat, which binds the patient's arms by crossing and tying them in front of their chest. While wearing this "straightjacket," a person would be unable to move the upper body, and would thus be safe from harm to himself and others. The straightjacket was sometimes also called the "MaddShirt."

sympathy—one certainly didn't treat a king like an animal, so why do so to those outside of the royal family? Reforms didn't immediately eliminate harsh treatments, though. People suffering from mental illness were often kept in poorhouses, asylums, and prisons under horrific conditions. It was not uncommon for patients to be restrained with chains or ropes. Order and control were the objectives; empathy and kindness were not.

The Committed at Pennsylvania Hospital

At Pennsylvania Hospital, a male cell keeper kept watch over the committed. This was a position that experienced high turnover—presumably owing both to the challenges of the job and to the fact that so many of the keepers also found it a convenient place to drink (and were promptly fired for doing so). Maintaining order and discipline was a keeper's most important task—even if it meant whipping or beating patients into submission. Despite the constant watch, it was common for the mentally ill to escape. Samuel Coates, Pennsylvania Hospital's manager from 1785–1825, recorded and commented on the escapades of mental patients:

> Polly—I believe it is forty years since this beautiful Girl first was brought to the Pennsylvania Hospital. Her insanity was attributed to disappointment in Love.
> One Night She was chained to the floor and to her Ancle in bed; in this situation with a saw or file, she separated the link next to her skin. This secret She kept

to herself, and continued in bed, holding in her hands the Ends of her chains.

In the morning, Doctor Hutchinson, passing her Cell door, She called to him & requested a favour, that he would shut the Window, for She was chilly. The Doctor immediately mounted a chair & drew the Sash down, but turning his Back instead of his face to the patient, She slyly Slipt out of bed, &, before he could dismount from his high Station, She was out, & bolting him in, escaped: there he was detained the best part of an hour, calling on Tom, Dick, or Harry, any one he cou'd see to deliver him from Prison.

The hue and Cry for Polly was soon made; at length she was found, wading up to her knees in Mud & water, thro' the mouth of the Culvert or common Sewer, into the Dock, nearly opposite to Joshua Gilpin's house. Where She first entered into this Subterranean passage, I do not remember, tho' I recollect her returning in high Glee to her old quarters, Exulting in the trick she had played upon the doctor.

Polly was not alone in seeking to escape. Hospital patients Jonathan Jones and Charles Jenkins were particularly skilled at such jailbreaks. They found the most success by forcing apart the iron bars in their cells and squeezing their way to freedom. The two ran away seven times, after which point a blacksmith was brought in to reinforce both men's cells. Jenkins was returned to the hospital at the request of the mayor, who worried for the lives of his wife and children as Jenkins was "abusive and Outragious." Despite his cell's reinforcement, Jenkins succeeded in escaping again, apparently occupying his free time with alcohol, and returned to the hospital "in a state of Drunken madness."

For nine years, an inmate (and former sailor) by the name of Thomas Perrine lived up in the hospital's small dome after escaping from his room. Perrine was reportedly a difficult patient who argued with the cell keeper and his fellow patients, finally retreating to the dome to live there until his death. Said the hospital managers

Packard v. Packard, 1864

In 1860, Reverend Theophilus Packard committed his wife, Elizabeth Packard (1816-1897), to Illinois' Jacksonville Insane Asylum for her "obnoxious" religious views that supposedly "were dangerous to the spiritual interests of his children and the community." In reality, Elizabeth vociferously disagreed with her more religiously conservative husband. The two were married for twenty-one years and had six children together.

Mrs. Packard spent three years at the asylum and, when moved back into her own home because of the "inability" to cure her of her insanity, her husband locked her in the nursery, nailing the windows shut! At the time, Illinois law (along with other states') allowed a husband to put his wife away without evidence of insanity or consent. Mrs. Packard found a legal loophole that a wife could not be put away in her own home. Elizabeth Packard took her husband to court and, after a seven-minute jury deliberation, she was declared sane, thus freed from confinement.

Estranged from her husband for the remainder of her life, Packard published books about her experience, founded the Anti-Insane Asylum Society, and advocated across the country for the rights of women, especially those alleged to be insane.

of Perrine, "He never left these cramped quarters for any purpose; he was also noted for his long nails, matted beard and hair and for his insensibility to cold, since he never, in the coldest weather of nine winters, came near to a fire."

Early on, mental patients were a source of entertainment for the public, who frequently spied on the patients and teased them through their cells' iron bars. To get rid of the annoying spectators, in 1760 hospital managers proposed "That a suitable Pallisade Fence, either of Iron or Wood, the Iron being preferr'd, should be erected in Order to prevent the Disturbance which is given to the Lunatics confin'd in the Cells by the great Numbers of people who frequently resort and converse with them. . . ." When completed, however, the iron fence did little to reduce onlookers. A small charge for viewings was devised as a possible solution for decreasing the number of gawkers. In 1784, the hospital's board created a rule that no more than two people could enter a patient's cell, with no talking permitted.

But it wasn't until 1791 that the privacy and safety of the mentally ill at Pennsylvania Hospital became a priority:

> That no Person whatever should be hereafter allowed to enter the Grounds, or Cells inclosed for their Accommodation unless introduced or allowed by one of the Managers, Physicians or by the Steward, to which resolution the Cell-Keeper was strictly to Attend, and to keep the Gates and Wards locked in future, to prevent all Intruders who might attempt to enter therein, without such permission being first obtained.

Given that most colonial Americans had little regard for and understanding of the mentally ill, mental patients at Pennsylvania Hospital received relatively kind care, much of which was under the direction of "the Father of American Psychiatry," Dr. Benjamin Rush (1745–1813), whose own son was a mental patient there.

Pennsylvania Hospital managers hired Dr. Rush in 1783, and he served the hospital until his death. Though many during the era believed mental illness was brought on by outside forces—by which people meant everything from tobacco to the bogey man—Rush

Personal Experience

Benjamin Rush's eldest son, John Rush, graduated from medical school, but left the profession behind when he joined the navy. After killing his good friend Benjamin Taylor in a duel (reasons unknown), John Rush attempted suicide and was admitted to Pennsylvania Hospital in 1810. He lived there until he died, twenty-seven years later. Benjamin Rush observed that his son returned from the navy as a man overcome with grief, unkempt, with long hair and a beard. Despite their pleas, John refused to talk to his family.

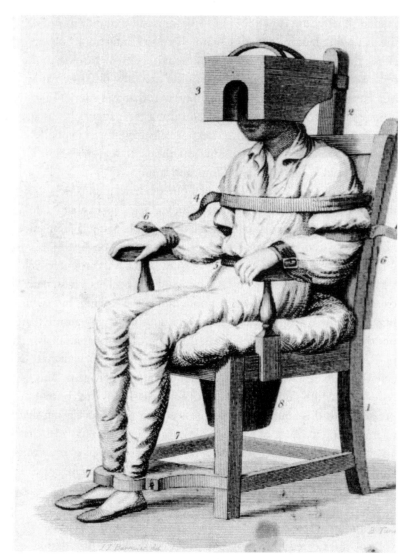

RUSH'S TRANQUILIZING CHAIR, COURTESY OF THE LIBRARY OF CONGRESS

suspected their sickness was caused by a disease of the brain. That's not to say that he didn't have his own set of questionable theories regarding causes: lovesickness, excessive drinking, and excessive religious fervor, for example. The influence of any of these conditions might very well bring on a change in behavior, but is certainly not the root cause of a mental illness. (Though not entirely understood, mental illnesses are now thought to be caused by one or more of the following factors: genetics, brain chemistry, infections, substance abuse, trauma and stress, and environmental hazards.) Similar to the restraints used by other physicians on the mentally ill in the name of a cure, Rush devised a tranquilizing chair that was supposed to reduce blood flow to the brain by confining the patient's limbs and head, thus providing a calming effect. (Claustrophobia, anyone?). Rush also employed other common methods such as starvation, extreme cold, gagging, blindfolding, and spinning.

Rush did request that the hospital put a stop to public viewings, and end the practice of binding mental patients in chains. He believed in giving menial tasks to relatively stable patients (a practice now known as occupational therapy). Some of the suggested jobs included weaving, gardening, cutting straw, and basic carpentry. Entertainment recommended by Rush included: checkers, chess, field trips, listening to music, riding a hobby horse, see-sawing, and swinging. All of these proposed activities were unusual during a time that put those with mental afflictions in the same category as animals.

Rush also advocated for the "close stool," a type of chair that acted as a toilet with an enclosed chamber pot underneath. This reduced the filth and smell typical of the cells. Rush was so impressed with this contraption that he went on record declaring that its inventor, Dr. Clark of England, deserved the same accolades that a scientist would receive for discovering a planet. Despite some outlandish ideas, Rush's innovations offered vast improvements for the physical conditions for mental patients.

Sadly, these gains didn't gain much traction elsewhere.

Ultimately, those with severe mental illness continued to be viewed and treated like animals until the mid-1900s. And despite Rush's efforts, America continued to lag far behind Europe. ●

Part Two

TWO STEPS FORWARD, ONE STEP BACK

Chapter 6
WANTED: MEDICAL PROFESSIONALISM

Dr. Rush and other similarly educated physicians were the medical leaders of colonial and post-revolution America, with Philadelphia firmly established as the epicenter of medicine. At the time of the American Revolution, only 400 out of the approximately 3,500 practicing physicians held medical degrees. That being said, medical degrees could easily be bought at graduation, so degrees didn't necessarily have today's equivalent value. It's unclear how many of those with degrees actually attended classes and participated in apprenticeships, versus those who simply paid for the diploma. The visionary Philadelphia physician, John Morgan (1735–1789), led the charge to improve American medical education and the profession as a whole. Said Morgan of his fellow physicians:

> Great is the havock which his [physician's] ignorance spreads on every side, robbing the affectionate husband of his darling spouse, or rendering the tender wife a helpless widow; increasing the number of orphans; mercilessly depriving them of their parent's support; bereaving the afflicted parents of their only comfort and hope, by the untimely death of their beloved infants, and laying whole families desolate. Remorseless foe to mankind! actuated by more than savage cruelty! hold thy exterminating hand.

From Surgery to Dancing

Tension with College of Philadelphia's medical professors, plus overflowing classrooms, led surgeon George McClellan (1797–1847) to become a teacher and ultimately also found Philadelphia's second medical school, Jefferson Medical College, in 1824. McClellan was fearless and exacting with his knife, described as a "born surgeon." As a youth, without any previous experience, McClellan successfully set and bandaged the fractured and hemorrhaging bone of his uncle's servant. It's said that McClellan once removed the lower part of a patient's jaw in four minutes. In his well-regarded, posthumously published 1848 book, *Principles and Practice of Surgery*, McClellan describes one of his many surgeries on a young woman who had a deep cut from a slate roof tile on the soul of her right foot:

> A long, broad, and deep transverse cicatrix [scar tissue] resulted, which in a few months became so tender and painful that she could not place the sole of that foot upon the floor, or bear the slightest pressure upon the scar. Several incisions had been made into it in ineffectual researches for what was supposed to be a portion of the slate broken off and retained in the center of the scar. The young lady was finally brought to me for treatment, and I excised the whole cicatrix [scar tissue] ... I had to cut through ... before I could get away the whole tumor. It proved to be a perfect gristle, and not a particle of broken slate could be found within its substance.

McClellan succeeded where others failed. The wound healed completely and McClellan reported that the patient was dancing just a month later with no hindrance.

John Morgan elaborately analyzed and criticized fellow medical students and physicians, inadvertently snubbing many of his peers who took his comments personally. The speech, which kicked off the College of Philadelphia's medical program, took place at the

Bumbershoot

Most of the 3,500 physicians at work during the revolutionary period made house calls, which meant walking the streets and battling the elements. Morgan was the first to use an umbrella in making his rounds, and was ridiculed by the press for doing so. (Hard-hitting news, right?) Umbrellas weren't considered masculine enough at the time—a rather silly notion, especially in an age before Gore-Tex. It wasn't long before other physicians ignored the teasing and followed Morgan's lead.

height of Morgan's popularity but, unfortunately for him, it also provoked an immediate and steep decline. Insulting an audience of one's peers by questioning their professionalism was not a smart career move. Morgan complained loudly—and frequently—about the inadequate apprenticeship system, pointing out that grooming a horse wasn't necessary to curing medical afflictions. He spouted from the soapbox of medical specialization, hoping to prevent physicians from engaging in the duties of surgeons, and vice versa. Until the late 1800s, specializing wasn't the norm. Morgan practiced what he preached: While at Pennsylvania Hospital, he did not perform any surgeries.

Physician vs. Physician

In 1766, John Morgan put his beliefs into practice and co-founded, with William Shippen, Jr., in 1766, the first colonial medical school at the College of Philadelphia (later called the University of Pennsylvania). Technically, Shippen started an independent medical program before Morgan, but Morgan alone took all of the credit for this achievement, which created an intense rivalry with his former friend. (The two showed the wisdom of the old saying about never going into business with friends or family.)

During the Revolutionary War, the spat between Morgan and Shippen became even uglier after Morgan was appointed the director-general of the army's Boston hospital. Like many at the top, Morgan was blamed for any and all failures when, in fact, Morgan was facing already existing problems of limited medical supplies and internal politics. Shippen became the most vociferous of Morgan's critics, and eventually Morgan was fired. And who replaced Morgan? Of course it was his nemesis, Shippen.

Morgan was outraged and wrote an account to Congress in his defense (clocking in at 140-plus pages), which helped prove that Shippen had used hospital supplies for his own economic gain, and also neglected soldiers) but ultimately did not harm Shippen's career. Several years later, Congress issued an official apology to Morgan, but it was too little, too late.

The squabbles of Morgan and Shippen drained Morgan's health and had the additional effect of derailing his efforts to improve American medicine. Benjamin Rush, upon hearing that his friend was ill, reported:

> This afternoon I was called to visit Dr. Morgan, but found him dead in a small hovel, surrounded with books and papers, on a light dirty bed. He was attended only by a washerwoman, one of his tenants. His niece, Polly Gordon, came in time enough to see him draw his last breath. His disorder was the influenza, but he had been previously debilitated by many other disorders. What a change from his former rank and prospects in Life! The man who once filled half the world with his name, had now scarcely friends enough left to bury him.

Morgan died with most of his professional dreams of medical specialization and improved education unrealized.

The College of Physicians of Philadelphia

A few years before his death, though, Morgan did successfully establish a medical guild much like the British Royal College of Physicians (RCP). Founded in 1518, the RCP administered an examination and, depending on the results, granted licenses to deserving apothecaries and physicians; it also punished those guilty of malpractice. In 1787, the College of Physicians of Philadelphia was created by Philadelphia's top physicians, who were then concerned with improving the level of professionalism and knowledge

Mütter Matters

Philadelphia physician Dr. Thomas Dent Mütter thought that a medical collection was crucial to the education of physicians, and amassed almost 1,400 medical objects and specimens to that end. That's dedication—or evidence of a hoarding problem, depending on your perspective. Mütter also used his collection while teaching: In the absence of rigorous scientific study and readily available cadavers, his specimens provided exposure to normal and diseased bones, organs, fetuses, and more.

A famously vain man, Mütter loved fashion, traveled the streets of Philadelphia in a gray carriage with a matching gray horse, and changed his last name from the common-sounding *Mutter* to the German word for mother, *Mütter*. Reconstructive surgery was one of Mutter's specialties, especially plastic surgery of the cleft palate, clubfoot, and other disfigurements. (A cleft palate and/or cleft lip is a birth defect in which there is either an opening from the roof of the mouth to the nose, or a gap between the upper lip that can extend up to the nose. Also a birth defect, a clubfoot is twisted so that it turns inward and down.)

Physical abnormalities were especially unsettling during the image-conscious Victorian era; Mutter's surgical skills provided great

THOMAS DENT MÜTTER, COURTESY OF THE NATIONAL LIBRARY OF MEDICINE

relief to his patients—allowing them to walk the streets again without enduring stares and whispers. Mütter supplemented his physician's income with teaching. He was an engaging professor, by all accounts, popular with students who were charmed by his wit and enthusiasm for the topic. His lectures also often included specimens from his collection. A fellow professor at Jefferson College said of Mütter, "He surrounded himself richly with materials of illustrations to excite, surprise and [inspire] wonder."

In 1858, the College of Physicians of Philadelphia and Dr. Mütter agreed to establish a museum, which combined its small number of specimens with his own. They made provisions for a fireproof brick building for the collection, and established a $30,000 endowment for a dedicated curator, lecturer, and funds to expand the collection. Just three months before his death from tuberculosis in 1859, Mütter gifted to the College of Physicians of Philadelphia his collection of specimens. An 1863 inventory recorded 474 bones, 215 wet preparations (parts preserved in jars), 200 casts, 20 wax models, 8 papier-maché models, 5 dried specimens, and 4 oil and 376 watercolor paintings. The Mütter Museum was born. And the College of Physicians of Philadelphia, an institution dedicated to tradition, did a fine job of preserving and growing the collection.

within the medical community. Specifically, the College of Physicians of Philadelphia existed "to advance the Science of Medicine, and thereby lessen human misery, by investigating the diseases and remedies which are peculiar to our country." Good intentions indeed, but without the overlap of science and medicine, as well as improved professional education and accountability, this small group of influential physicians could not accomplish much. It would take many decades for real, large-scale change to happen.

Members of the College of Physicians of Philadelphia gained a medical library of the highest standards, as well as the ability to learn from other members through lectures and meetings. John Morgan was the first to gift the library his medical collection, including a very important work by the previously mentioned Italian physician Morgagni. The College of Physicians of Philadelphia frequently advised city officials on diseases, drugs, public sanitation, and more.

From its inception, it was a class-conscious organization in which old-timers nominated future members. Nepotism at its finest. The founders were part of Philadelphia's medical elite and were not known for their eagerness to adopt new ideas, but this reluctance to embrace change was at least a benefit to the preservation of both its medical library and museum (if not to progress). ✷

Chapter 7

CUT 'EM UP IN THE NAME OF EDUCATION

Mütter and his peers recognized just how crucial it was to include dissection and the study of human remains in educating future physicians. During the eighteenth and nineteenth centuries of American medicine, medical cadavers were educational gold. Reverend John Todd, once a physician's apprentice, recorded in his diary a need for a human skeleton. Upon hearing of a hunter buried in the woods, Todd and his partner-in-crime traveled 250 miles over two weeks to retrieve the body. Said Todd of their find:

> How I found the poor stranger's grave and exulted as a miser would have done over gold, and how I worked and toiled and finally got the bones, every one of them! into my bag and on my back, I shall not attempt to describe. It cost me three days' hard work, and work not the most pleasant. . . . but how I gloated over those bones! studied them! strung them! They were the beginnings of my professional knowledge and were worth to me a thousand fold more than their cost.

Although dramatic, Todd's sentiment captures the value of human remains to the medical student and physician.

Public Protests

The public's opposition to human dissection was a major obstacle to improving medicine and the overall quality of care. This attitude can be traced back to the Greeks, who believed that the human body should be respected after death. For centuries, Western medicine didn't recognize that studying dead bodies could be of real benefit to the living. Dissection was also generally not practiced in India or China, and was forbidden in Islamic medicine.

A FLEEING GRAVE ROBBER, COURTESY OF THE NATIONAL LIBRARY OF MEDICINE

During the 1788 "Doctors' Mob," angry rioters in New York City tried to murder doctors who were known to be teaching human dissection. The situation is supposed to have begun when a medical student used a dissected arm to wave at a group of boys. According to one account, one of the boys was told that the arm was from his recently deceased mother. When the boy's father heard that his wife's grave may have been robbed, he led a group of men through the dissection room, destroying everything. Over the course of three days, the army was summoned to protect the physicians, who were then mostly in hiding. In the end, eight demonstrators were killed, and the anatomical museum of Drs. Bayley and Clossy was destroyed.

This was not an isolated incident. In 1824, another mob of about six hundred men attacked Yale's medical school with guns, clubs, and daggers upon learning that a nearby grave had been robbed of its contents for the purpose of dissection.

Questionable Methods

Philadelphia anatomist Joseph Leidy was responsible for obtaining at least two bodies through questionable methods, both of which ended up at the Mütter Museum. One of the specimens is the "Soap Lady," a woman whose fatty tissue in her decomposed body turned into a waxy substance similar to that of soap. Dr. Joseph McFarland, a curator from the museum, wrote that the Soap Lady was "one of the most revolting objects that can be imagined."

The body was supposedly discovered when a Philadelphia cemetery's burial plots were moved from one location to another; Leidy acquired the body and donated it to the museum. But in reading between the lines of the Soap Lady's documentation, it's clear that Leidy used shady means to obtain the body: He pretended to be a relative, wrote on paper a fictitious name for the woman, said her body had been located at a cemetery that didn't actually exist, and fabricated the year (1792) and cause of her death (yellow fever). Leidy kept all information about her true identity a secret, but hinted at his dubious methods on the receipt of her purchase: "the above amount is one-half of the sum paid persons through whose connivance I was enabled to procure two adipocere (waxy) bodies, one for the College of Physicians the other for the University." "Connivence..." aka bribery.

An X-ray of the body in 1987 revealed that the pins holding together the cloth she was buried in were from the first half of the 1800s, confirming the deliberate misinformation. Leidy was clearly worried that someone, probably the Soap Lady's family, would learn the truth.

Leidy also bought a giant skeleton from Kentucky for $50. At 7' 6", it was the largest skeleton on public display in North America. Leidy made arrangements for the skeleton under the condition that no attempts be made to identify the origins of the body, almost certainly indicating that—like the Soap Lady—the American Giant was purchased illegally.

The giant's spine was very curved, reducing his actual height. The Royal College of Surgeons in England has the tallest skeleton in the world, that of Charles Byrne, who was 7' 7". The Mütter skeleton was in his twenties when he died; from an examination of his skull and certain abnormalities, it appears that he suffered from gigantism, caused by an overactive pituitary gland producing too much growth hormone. The reason for this overproduction is often a noncancerous tumor of the pituitary gland, a very rare condition. Today, gigantism can be treated with either surgery or medication.

Dead Bodies By Any Means Necessary

The inability of nineteenth-century American and European physicians to legally acquire cadavers often led to shady methods. "Resurrectionists" or "sack-'em up men" were professionals employed in the business of robbing graves—no previous experience required. Bodies were priced by size, adults labeled "larges" and children as "smalls." The public went to great measures to protect graves from body snatchers: iron bars and fences, locked coffins, cemetery guards, and large stones placed upon fresh graves. But the money earned from corpses outweighed the risks. In some places, a fresh body paid as much as a field hand could earn in a year.

In the most extreme case, William Burke and William Hare in Scotland murdered guests at their hotel in order to obtain bodies to sell for dissection at Robert Knox's anatomy school. Suffocation was their method of choice. A charming ditty of unknown authorship about Burke and Hare went like this:

> *Burke's the Butcher,*
> *Hare's the Thief,*
> *Knox the man who buys the Beef.*

Burke and Hare are said to have killed at least sixteen people in total. Eventually Hare ratted on Burke, who was then tried, convicted, and hanged. Burke's body was then dissected and put on display for the public; his skeleton rests in the Edinburgh University Medical School today. How fitting.

Students were strictly forbidden from talking about classroom dissections for fear of revealing the source of the cadavers. Once a body was obtained (by means fair or foul—usually foul), the dissection would proceed according to the decomposition rate of the various parts, with the guts and organs (the quickest to degenerate) done first and the muscles and skeleton (the most enduring parts) done last. Some anatomists even encouraged their medical students to taste a cadaver's bodily fluids. Gross. . . and dangerous.

It was often the poor and disenfranchised whose bodies were dug up from graves or taken from poorhouses—existing prejudices making the desecration easier to defend. The New Orleans Charity Hospital greatly benefitted from its location in a busy seaport, which attracted a constant influx of newly arrived laborers (aka "fresh meat"). Many of those who died in the hospital were poor and not originally from New Orleans, with the result that there would be no family members to claim the body. Easy access to cadavers was even a point of advertisement for New Orleans' various medical schools.

All this being said, more widespread human dissection would have done much to increase the education of physicians in their fairly limited understandings of the human body. As a London surgeon put it, "Without dissection there can be no anatomy. . . I would not remain in a room with a man who attempted to perform an operation in surgery who was unacquainted with anatomy. . . . he must mangle the living if he has not operated on the dead." •

Chapter 8
EVERYONE WANTS TO BE A HERO

Greek taboos prevented human dissection, yet Hippocrates, "the father of medicine," managed to provide medical insight. Hippocrates suggested that illnesses were caused by nature, not by the whims of the gods (a major step forward). Fortunately, his theory stuck—as did his code, which instilled the motto that doctors still subscribe to and seek to abide by today—"first, do no harm." It was thought during the Hippocratic era of medicine that airborne vapors—the Greek word was *miasma*, meaning to pollute—caused fevers and diseases. The disgusting smells from swampy areas were seen as evidence of dangerous air.

The Four Humors

One of Hippocrates' lasting medical concepts, humorism, divided the body into four sections based on different types of bodily fluids: black bile, yellow bile, blood, and phlegm—commonly known as "humors."

> The body of man has in itself blood, phlegm, yellow bile, and black bile; these make up the nature of the body, and through these he feels pain or enjoys health. Now, he enjoys the most perfect health when these elements are duly proportioned to one another in respect to compounding, power and bulk, and when they are

perfectly mingled. Pain is felt when one of these elements is in defect or excess, or is isolated in the body without being compounded with all the others.

"Humor" is translated from the Greek *chymos*, meaning juice or sap. Each humor corresponded to an organ and a particular season: blood with the heart and spring; yellow bile with the liver and summer; black bile with the spleen and autumn; and phlegm with the brain and winter. There were personality characteristics associated with each humor: courageous and playful (blood); thoughtful and patient (phlegm); ambitious and easily angered (yellow bile); and serious and analytical (black bile). Black bile was considered the cause of the gravest illnesses. It was supposed that the balance of these four humors was essential for a healthy body.

Prophetic Pee

From uroscopy came the bizarre practice of uromancy, telling one's fortune from the bubbles and color of one's pee. Uromancers—or "piss prophets"—would pour a customer's urine into a special glass bowl and hold the bowl up to the light to remark on the color. Special attention was paid to the number of bubbles.

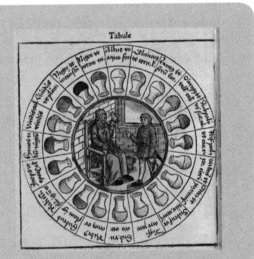

GUIDE TO ANALYZING URINE, COURTESY OF THE LIBRARY OF CONGRESS

Large bubbles spread far apart meant that a financial success would be imminent. Small bubbles close together were bad news. Some expectant mothers visited a piss prophet to learn the sex of their baby. The long robes worn by the uromancers lent the practice an air of mystery. (Practically speaking, it's what one eats and drinks, as well as medications, that determine urine color.)

Physicians in ancient Greece would even go so far as to taste their patient's urine or earwax to determine if the humors were out of whack. Sweet earwax implied death, whereas a bitter flavor suggested recovery. The practice of studying a patient's urine—"uroscopy," as it was known—continued to be used into the mid-nineteenth century, though it was largely ineffective. The height of its popularity was the Middle Ages.

Galen's Influence

Galen (129–201), a Roman physician during the second century and physician to Roman Emperor Marcus Aurelius, codified the Hippo-cratic humors in a quasi-scientific way, with particular attention to the functions of each specific body part. He considered his work to be the definitive study of the body and its imbalances, a legacy that lasted more than 1,500 years, much to the detriment of medicine.

Galen is reported to have employed twenty scribes to record his medical dictations, clocking in at an estimated five to ten million words in total. One surviving bit of wisdom from Galen includes this: "Every animal is sad after coitus (sexual intercourse), except the human female and the rooster." It's not clear why Galen believed that this bizarre observation deserved inclusion in any medical trea-tise, but such thoughts—along with his other works—were kept and preserved thanks to the translations of Arabic physicians. At the time that Europe was in the Dark Ages (600s to 1400s), Arab medicine flourished with the successes of Al-Rhazi, Avicenna, and Ibn Sina. Scholar Hunayn ibn Ishāq translated so many texts that his nick-name was the "sheikh of translators."

Galen learned about human anatomy by tending to Roman gladiators and their horrific wounds, and dissecting dogs, pigs, and monkeys. He supposedly enjoyed demonstrations of live dissections of pigs—called vivisections—in which the pig only stopped squeal-ing when Galen sliced its neck. Renowned anatomist and physician Vesalius (1514–1564) rebelled against Galen's teachings, arguing, "Galen was deceived by his monkeys." Vesalius's rebellion was rather bold and few joined his protests. Because of Vesalius's work with skeletons and the human body, he knew Galen's purported medi-cal knowledge based solely on animal dissections was riddled with mistaken information. Though there are anatomical similarities among mammals, ultimately the differences between humans and Galen's animals led to errors. Most of his errors are reflected in his theories of blood circulation, in which the liver played an important role in consuming and regenerating blood. In reality, the liver's function is centered on metabolism. Unfortunately, Galen's suppositions prevailed, especially his theory of humorism.

Balancing the Humors

From Hippocrates onward, it was thought that reducing an of-fending humor through bleeding, blistering, and/or purging was the best cure for almost any illness. Bleeding—or bloodletting, or "breathing the vein," or "phlebotomy," or "venesection"—was the most popular method, traditionally done three different ways: via cutting, leeches, or cupping. Bloodletting has a history of 3,000 years, beginning in Egypt. Early bloodletting was done as a simple cut using thorns, roots, fish teeth, or sharpened rocks. The most common method relied on a lancet to cut the vein at the elbow. The use of a lancet wound inspired an 1841 poem, with the title "To My Spring-Lancet," part of which reads:

> I love thee, bloodstain'd, faithful friend
> As warrior loves his sword or shield;
> For how on thee did I depend
> When foes of Life were in the field!

> Those blood spots on thy visage, tell
> That thou, thro horrid scenes, hast past.
> O, thou hast served me long and well;
> And I shall love thee to the Last!

Such devotion. The spring lancet was especially popular with American physicians. A bowl was usually employed to capture the patient's spurting blood. The physician pulled the bloody bowl at just the right time so as not to spill a single drop, an indication of the physician's expertise of when the vein was adequately drained. Bloodletting was so popular at the time that some did it habitually during certain times of the year, such as during allergy season. Calendars were marked to indicate the more favorable days for bloodletting.

Leeches were the second bloodletting method of choice. Placed on various parts of the body, leeches were starved to encourage biting and

LEECH THERAPY, COURTESY OF THE NATIONAL LIBRARY OF MEDICINE

sucking. Leeches range in size, with the smallest being one-quarter of an inch. Bloodsucking leeches expand to five to six times their original size after a feeding, despite only sucking about a teaspoon of blood. Before feeding, a thread was tied through a leech's tail to fish it out if it traveled into a patient's body, An illustration from an Egyptian tomb in the second millennium BCE shows an early example of bloodletting with leeches. At one point, there was such a large demand for leeches in France that there were leech farms. Women were hired to collect leeches by exposing their bare legs in ponds.

The last method of bloodletting was cupping, either dry or wet. Dry cupping involved no blood and was the application of a cup that was used to suction part of the skin to create swelling. Once dry cupping was applied, wet cupping might follow. A small incision was made and, again, a cup was used to catch the blood. This method varied from venesection in that the cuts weren't applied to a vein. If a physician surmised that a patient couldn't handle cutting a vein because of weakness or age, cupping was used. Cupping fell out of favor in the early 1800s, and leeches in the 1830s.

Another method for balancing the humors was blistering, which involved applying a harsh substance to the skin that elicited a second-degree burn. The burn was then inflamed and infected by applying hot packs. The resulting inflammation and pus was thought to be a sign of healing. (In actuality, it is a sign of infection.) Ouch!

Lastly, purging was accomplished through forced vomiting or diarrhea. A country physician observed of purging: "If vomited, they did not come up in gentle puffs and gusts, but the action was cyclonic. If, perchance, the stomach was passed the expulsion would be by the rectum and anus, and this would be equal to a regular oil-well gusher."

Enemas were also particularly popular in Renaissance France. King Louis XIII, for instance—the man who ruled France from 1610 to 1643—received 212 enemas and forty-seven bleedings in one year.

To "bleed, blister, and purge" was deemed heroic therapy because of "the strength of its combined actions." And after bleeding and purging, tonics (consisting of arsenic and other deadly ingredients) were administered as a "cure." Pick your poison.

The harsh treatments of heroic medicine were administered to an American population that wasn't particularly healthy. Most didn't bathe more than a couple of times a year, and soap was not affordable. The working class and the poor of early 1800s America lived in the midst of sewage, polluted water, unhygienic living conditions, poor nutrition, and pests, which all contributed to their susceptibility to illness. Bleeding, blistering, and purging an already fragile constitution did little to ensure healing and recovery. Patients expected heroic medicine to work, but to the extent that it did, it was evidence more of the power of the placebo than the power of bloodletting itself. Positive thinking may be the cure, but the heroic method rarely was.

The heroic method stood the test of time, however, up until the mid-1800s, because physicians didn't have a solid understanding of diseases and their causes. And that wasn't the only problem: Medical instruments were crude at best, and the concept of infection was a foreign one. Fever was an all-inclusive description for an imbalance in the body, and bloodletting was the dominant treatment. The harm done in the name of medicine through bloodletting was immeasurable. Medical historian Ira Rutkow explains, "Doctors bled some patients sixteen ounces a day up to fourteen days in succession (the average male human body contains 175 ounces of blood)." Compare this to today's standards of giving blood, in which a donor is limited to sixteen ounces per session, with a mandatory waiting period of *two* months between sessions. ●

Chapter 9
WHAT A RUSH

The previously mentioned Dr. Benjamin Rush took the theory of humorism and ran with it. Rush was especially aggressive when it came to bleeding, blistering, puking, and purging. Colonial Quaker Elizabeth Drinker's 1807 diary entries recorded the heroic medical treatment of her husband, Henry Drinker:

Sept. 1, 1807: 'My husband's disorder has turn'd on his bowels as usual, he has been very often this day moved and has taken 40 drops liquid ladunum[1] going to bed

Sep. 2. . . My husband very unwell in his bowels, he voids blood in his stools, sent for Dr. Rush this even. who ordred a blister applied to his side. supposing he has something of ye Pleurisey[2], but to me it appears to be a kidney complaint, we applied the blister, and gave him 100 drops of asthmatic Elexer[3]. . .

Sep. 3. . . Dr. Rush visited my husband he advised another bleeding which was done, 8 ounces was taken by John Uhlehe also advis'd rice water, and an injection at going to bed, of flaxceed tea a gill, and 40 drops liquid [ladunum], all which was done

---

1. A popular and highly addictive opium tincture often prescribed by physicians of the time.
2. Inflammation of the lungs that causes chest pain.
3. Antiquated spelling of elixir, meaning a potion.

Sep. 4... My husband has been unwell all day, he was let
blood y 3. day successively: John Hule bleed him—he
has took little or no nourishment for 2 or 3 days past...

Sep. 5... Dr. Rush came he ask'd me what I thought
of my husband losing 6 ounces more blood, he
was sure it was necessary... he ordered 6 or 8 more
ounces more taken, which was accordingly done—
and it appears worse than any yet taken from him...

It wasn't until a month later that Henry Drinker was well enough
to resume his normal life, probably relieved to leave the extreme
bleeding and blistering of Rush behind.

Extreme Bloodletting

Rush first established his reputation at Pennsylvania Hospital during
the yellow fever epidemic of 1793. Rush did this by remaining in
the city to care for the infected. It was probably a coincidence, but
the first patients who Rush treated with his regimen survived. Rush
claimed that, of the one hundred people who he'd visited or treated
for yellow fever in one day, none died. Unknown to physicians at
the time, the cause of yellow fever is a virus spread by mosquitos,
attended by symptoms of aches, jaundice (yellowing of the skin and
eyes), fever, vomiting, and, if untreated, organ failure, coma, seizure,
and hemorrhaging.

In desperation, people shot at the miasma (bad air) because they
believed gunpowder warded off the yellow fever, but all this led to was
Philadelphia's mayor outlawing gunpowder because so many were injured. Rush theorized that coffee dumped and rotting in Philadelphia's
harbor caused yellow fever. At the end of the epidemic, more than 10
percent of the population had died (about four thousand people), and
another twenty thousand people had fled the city as a result.

By 1800, Benjamin Rush was commonly considered to be the
greatest American physician. Presidents James Monroe and John
Adams consulted with him on the health of their own daughters.
Rush also lectured to several thousand would-be doctors, which
popularized the heroic method in America and added to the image

of Philadelphia as the country's leading medical center. His writings and teachings were littered with conclusions based on his experiences. Anecdotal evidence was the practice *du jour* by physicians before and after Rush. A key phrase used by Rush in his defense was "my view establishes that. . ." and he would leave it at that. Try that on your next homework assignment.

Despite his title and reputation, Rush made terrible conclusions for the medical world. He mistakenly believed that four-fifths of a patient's blood should be drained to relieve excitement in the veins, which he saw as the sole cause of disease. Unfortunately, Rush's calculations overestimated the amount of blood in the human body. He thought people had about twenty-five pounds' worth of blood, when in fact we have closer to twelve. And his back-up method when bloodletting wasn't enough? Purging and blistering. Rush had his own pill concoction known as *thunderclappers*—so-called because of their dramatic impact—which even accompanied Lewis and Clark on their expedition. "Dr. Rush's Bilious Pills," as they were formally known, were strong laxatives that contained so much mercury that historians were able to trace the expedition's trail based on the high levels of metal in their poop. Rush and others also administered calomel, which has a high level of mercury; this caused vomiting and/or diarrhea. (Patients paid for this!) When the mercury from calomel reached high levels in the body, the resulting side effects included teeth falling out, a rotting jaw, ulcers, and other painful results. Dying sounds like a much better alternative.

Despite his popularity, Rush did have some detractors. Having a unique combination of geniality and egotism, Rush inspired either lifelong loyalty or extreme dislike among Philadelphia's prominent physicians. A few vehemently opposed Rush's drastic bloodletting during the yellow fever epidemic. When Rush learned of a peer's insults, he likened his opponent to Brutus, the man who helped assassinate Julius Caesar. Under most ethical codes, criticism and murder aren't on par.

The English writer William Cobbett tried to prove that Rush's bloodletting killed yellow fever patients by poring over Philadelphia's death records. Cobbett called Rush's zeal for heroic methods "one of the great discoveries which are made from time to time for the depopulation of the earth." After accusing Rush of killing

A Sickly President

We tend to imagine George Washington as a figure of commanding strength, a man who led a new country into its future, finally free from its oppressors. But like the citizens he led, Washington suffered from the same diseases that plagued so many others in the eighteenth and nineteenth centuries: diphtheria, smallpox, tuberculosis, dysentery, and malaria. (Hey, Washington managed to evade yellow fever, syphilis, and cholera, at least.) These days, diphtheria is prevented with a vaccine. The World Health Organization declared that smallpox had been eradicated in 1980. Dysentery and TB are now mostly contained with antibiotics. Unfortunately, we still struggle to eliminate deaths from malaria.

After a horse ride, Washington came down with a sore throat that developed into severe problems swallowing and breathing. What most likely killed Washington was epiglottitis, an extreme swelling of the flap at the back of the throat. Some modern physicians attribute his death to quinsy, an abscess behind the tonsils that causes swelling. Arguments aside, the malady occurred in the throat—that much at least was settled—and physicians applied dried beetles to Washington's neck in hopes of drawing out the throat infection. The physicians supposed that the swelling was due to an excess of blood, which resulted in Washington having 80 percent of his blood drained—an insurmountable volume, resulting in a painful death. A physician who argued against further bleeding of Washington,

people in a series of articles and pamphlets, Cobbett went so far as to blame Rush's teachings for the death of George Washington, who was, within twenty-four hours, bled—over a gallon!—by his Rush-trained physicians. Washington was only sick with a sore throat. Rush later sued Cobbett for libel and won. In reviewing Dr. Rush's papers and theories, Dr. Elisha Bartlett wrote in the 1840s, "In the whole vast compass of medical literature, there cannot be found an equal number of pages containing a greater amount and variety of utter nonsense and unqualified absurdity."

Eisha Cullen Dick, said, "He needs all his strength—bleeding will diminish it." Modern medical analysis suggests that a simple tracheotomy (a hole cut into the neck to create an airway directly into the windpipe) would have saved Washington's life.

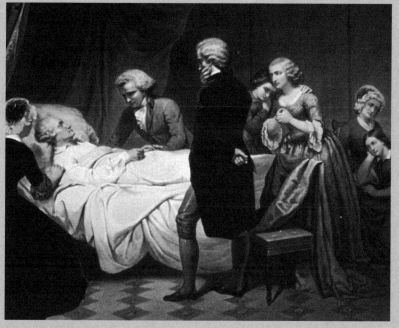

GEORGE WASHINGTON ON HIS DEATHBED, COURTESY OF THE NATIONAL LIBRARY OF MEDICINE

Despite detractors who questioned his overzealous approach to heroic medicine, Benjamin Rush's reputation thrived, and he wound up shaping the face of American medicine long after his death. Rush disciples spread his enthusiasm for extreme bloodletting across the country, drowning out any contrary opinions or new medical theories until late in the nineteenth century. Moderation was not the name of the game, and the American people paid with their lives. ✱

Chapter 10
THE OPERATION GAME

Like general medical practice, surgery was still developing in the early 1800s. Surgical anesthesia wasn't successfully administered until 1846 by William Morton and John Collins Warren, with sterilization applied several decades later by British surgeon Joseph Lister. Before the advent of both anesthesia and sterilization, operations were unbearably painful and dirty. In 1843, Professor George Wilson described his ankle amputation in the following terms:

> The horror of great darkness, and the sense of desertion by God and man, bordering close on despair. . . I can never forget, however gladly I would do so. During the operation, in spite of the pain it occasioned, my senses were preternaturally acute, as I have been told they generally are in patients in such circumstances. I still recall with unwelcome vividness the spreading out of the instruments: the twisting of the tourniquet: the first incision: the fingering of the sawed bone: the sponge pressed on the flap: the tying of the blood-vessels: the stitching of the skin: the bloody dismembered limb lying on the floor.

Fortunately for Professor Wilson, amputations were relatively common and quick. And though Wilson's surgeon was James Syme, the namesake for the procedure (a Syme amputation), amputations did not require a high level of skill and precision. The acuteness of a patient's pain during surgery meant that quickness was paramount.

Holes in the Head

Trepanning, the practice of drilling a hole into the skull and removing the bone, is one of the oldest known surgical techniques. It is not entirely clear why trepanning occurred thousands of years ago—some speculate that the hole was made to release spirits or demons from the head. Others attribute it to a ritualistic practice. A modern version of trepanation, more commonly called craniotomy, is used in the case of brain injuries. A bone flap is cut into the skull to provide temporary access to the brain. Unlike historical trepanning, surgeons use the hole to operate on or monitor the brain, replacing the removed skull as quickly as possible.

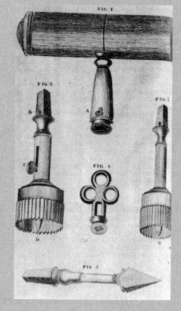

TREPHINING EQUIPMENT, COURTESY OF THE NATIONAL LIBRARY OF MEDICINE

Surgeries were often performed in front of an audience of medical students and the public, allowing for optimum teaching (and entertainment) opportunities. The first surgical amphitheater was built in 1803 at New York Hospital, and the second was constructed by Pennsylvania Hospital in 1804. Using an amphitheater as a formal teaching tool set surgery apart as a unique discipline, different enough from a physician's work to necessitate a distinct setting for education.

Without electric lights, the main source of light in Pennsylvania Hospital's amphitheater was a skylight, which meant that surgeries had to be performed during the brightest parts of the day. Audiences paid to watch as doctors amputated limbs, set broken bones, and removed tumors on patients who weren't anesthetized. (In many ways, surgical viewings in amphitheaters were the precursor to medical dramas, albeit significantly more horrific.) Until anesthesia, alcohol, drugs, or a knock upside the head were employed to render a patient unconscious, but "hopefully not dead." Patients were tied down and/or held down by men strong enough to prevent a patient from moving. The sounds of thrashing and screams filled medical amphitheaters.

Bloody Stripes

In Europe, barbers initially took on the role of surgeons because of the ancient belief that good and evil spirits entered the body through the hair on one's head. Plus, early physicians thought they were too sophisticated and educated to perform surgery. The red-and-white barber pole most likely originates from drying bandages outside of the barbershop, red from bloodletting. Eventually, the red and white striped pole became an advertisement for the barber-surgeon rather than the academic surgeon. A blue-and-white pole emerged in England in 1540 and indicated that the barber within could not do advanced surgery; those with red-and-white poles could do so, but were forbidden from cutting hair or shaving clients.

Surgical Survivors

There are a couple of surgical cases that stand out in early American medical history as the first of their kind. Ephraim McDowell (1771–1830) was an accomplished American surgeon who in 1809 operated on a woman believed to be pregnant with twins. Mrs. Jane Todd Crawford was not actually pregnant, but swollen from a tumor. At McDowell's urging, Crawford rode to McDowell's hometown—a full sixty miles on horseback—and then submitted herself to the surgical skills of McDowell and two assistants. McDowell chose Christmas Day for the operation. Crawford's abdomen was opened and the diseased ovary removed, weighing in at almost twenty pounds. Her intestines were out of her body for thirty minutes, after which McDowell bathed them in lukewarm water and then pushed them back into her body. Crawford sang hymns and repeated psalms during her surgery. Surprisingly, Crawford survived the ordeal and lived for another thirty-one years, dying at the ripe old age of seventy-eight. When news of Mrs. Jane Todd Crawford's operation by McDowell reached London, it was remarked "A back-settlement of America—Kentucky—has beaten the mother country, nay, Europe itself, with all the boasted surgeons thereof in the fearful and formidable operation of gastrostomy, with the extraction of diseased ovaria."

Another amazing surgical feat was performed by William Beaumont (1785–1853), a physician instrumental in discovering the nature of human digestion. In June of 1822, Alexis St. Martin, a French-Canadian trapper, was accidentally shot at close range with a shotgun and suffered from a very serious stomach wound. Beaumont used the hole, which had failed to close, as a means of accessing St. Martin's stomach. Through this passageway, Beaumont dropped food on a string, down and back up, for measured periods of time to observe the work of gastric juices. St. Martin left the doctor after three long years. (Just imagine, three years!)

After St. Martin's departure, Beaumont tracked him down and continued with experiments from 1829 to 1831. In 1832, Beaumont committed St. Martin to a contract, but by 1834, St. Martin had enough and refused to continue his guinea-pig role. In the end, however, Beaumont had gotten enough information to publish "Experiments and Observations on the Gastric Juice and the Physiology of Digestion" in 1833, a work essential to our understanding of digestion. At his death, St. Martin's family, sympathetic to all he

The Father of American Surgery

Dr. Philip Syng Physick (1768–1837), the "Father of American Surgery," had an impressive career at Pennsylvania Hospital. Physick initially questioned his career choice; fortunately for his eventual patients, his father forbade him to leave medicine. Physick was renowned for the steadiness of his hand and precision, especially as surgery progressed and became more complicated. Like Benjamin Rush, Physick was one of the few physicians who remained in Philadelphia during the yellow fever crisis.

Dr. Physick was known for seeking bodies for dissection. While working one day, Physick received a knock at the door, a delivery of a body. Unfortunately, it was the body of Physick's mentor, *the* Benjamin Rush. A shocker, to say the least. This prompted Physick to give specific instructions that when he died, his body should be kept in the family home for several months so that decomposition would render it useless for dissection.

POSTER ADVERTISING CHANG AND ENG, COURTESY OF THE NATIONAL LIBRARY OF MEDICINE

suffered for science, let his body rot and buried him in an unmarked grave so that he couldn't be dug back up for more experimentation. The medical profession owed much to the risk and sacrifice of Jane Todd Crawford and Alex St. Martin in a time of crude surgical conditions.

The medical case of Chang and Eng stumped surgeons. Chang and Eng were the source of the phrase *Siamese Twins* (a reference to their birthplace in Bangkok, Siam—now known as Thailand). Born in 1811, the twins were connected by a piece of tissue roughly at stomach level. They were brought to the United States in 1829 for the purpose of touring the country as an exhibit. For six weeks in 1860, Chang and Eng were part of a show at Barnum's American Museum. Throughout their lives, they consulted with surgeons to explore the possibility of separation, but no one could ever safely recommended the procedure because of surgical limitations. (Plus, it's reported that the two did not feel a need for separate bodies.) The first successful separation of conjoined twins was in 1689 by a Swiss surgeon; those twins were also linked at the abdomen.

Chang and Eng married sisters Sarah Ann and Adelaide Yaites in 1843 and arrived at the unusual routine of visiting their respective wives on alternating days. The two couples produced a total of twenty-one children! In 1871, Chang suffered a stroke and was paralyzed on his right side, which meant that Eng had to support part of his twin's weight. Compounding matters, Chang started to drink heavily. Three years later, in January of 1874, Chang contracted bronchitis, had trouble breathing, and died in his sleep. Unfortunately, the local physician arrived too late to separate the twins. Eng, complaining of a "choking sensation," died, most likely from a lack of blood flow.

Members of the College of Physicians of Philadelphia performed the twins' autopsy. Chang and Eng's families agreed to a plaster before burial, as well as the preservation of the twins' respective conjoined livers for display. The two would not have survived surgical separation. Two of their children wrote to a Philadelphia physician participating in their autopsy (April 1, 1874):

Dr. Allen

Enclosed you will find the receipt for bringing the bodies of Papa & uncle from Salem to our house. You will please send the money by post-office order.

My Mother and Aunt were very sorry that we did not bring the lungs and entrals [sic] of our Father's with the bodies home, and as we did not bring them, you may keep them until further orders from the families.

Respectfully G,R, & S,D, Bunker

In an age when the intricacies of the human body were somewhat of a mystery, restricting the ability of surgeons to perform precise and complicated operations, Chang and Eng's plaster and livers provided a tangible reminder of their limitations. •

Chapter 11
ALTERNATIVES TO HEROIC MEDICINE

It was during the 1830s that American patients became eager for alternatives to the heroic method of bleeding, blistering, puking, and purging. Established medicine was no great shakes, given that anyone could establish a medical school and hand out diplomas. Apprenticeships were of little benefit too, since any physician—no matter how incompetent—could take on a student for free labor and graduate him with no more than a superficial certificate. In practice, American physicians did not take a scientific approach.

The public's lack of faith in so-called medical experts was compounded by the politics of the time. President Andrew Jackson (in office 1829-1837) emphasized a philosophy of self-reliant individuals. This translated into an environment in which patients refused to be held hostage to a medical establishment and its heavy-handed billing practices. This coincided with exploding newspaper circulation, which provided endless advertising possibilities, as well as articles touting the miraculous cures provided by the latest and greatest tonic. Poor and rural populations were especially vulnerable to quackery.

The appeal of alternative medicine was hope. As wacky as some of these alternative therapies and fads may seem to us now, those offering less conventional forms of treatment weren't necessarily aiming to swindle their patients. Without a doubt, some quacks sought to take advantage of the public's gullibility in the name of a buck. But much like the sometimes curative powers of heroic medicine

POLITICAL CARTOON CRITICIZING PHYSICIANS, COURTESY OF THE NATIONAL LIBRARY OF MEDICINE

because of the placebo effect, a hopeful attitude toward alternatives could transform into a cure.

Homeopathy

One of the first alternatives on the scene was homeopathy, which is still in use today. Homeopathic founder Samuel Hahnemann (1755-1843) of Germany experimented on himself and other healthy individuals. Hahnemann believed that if a certain, diluted concoction mimicked the symptoms of a particular disease in a healthy person, then that same concoction could cure a sick person with that same disease by pushing it out of the body. Hahnemann penned an essay poking fun at the typical physician's house call:

> Doors fly open at his approach, three steps bring him to the patient's side. He feels his pulse, asks him a couple of questions, and without reply calls for pen, ink, and paper: and after deep reflection for two seconds in his chair he

suddenly dashes off the complex prescription, politely hands it to the patient... makes his bow and disappears, in order to be with another patient six seconds afterwards, on whom also he bestows his two minutes of advice.

After its start in Europe, homeopathy was introduced to America in 1825. The father of American homeopathy, Constantine Herring, experimented with snake venom as a cure, as well as the explosive nitroglycerin (a key ingredient in dynamite) for headaches. Hygiene, a healthy diet, and exercise, also went hand-in-hand with homeopathy. (So not all bad news.)

Because of its popularity among European aristocrats, homeopathy appealed to the middle and upper classes living in American cities as well. It helped that the homeopathic physicians were often highly educated. Conveniently, homeopathic cures tended to taste better and be cheaper than those given by the physicians and, at the very least, didn't do as much harm as, say, heroic medicine's poisonous mercury. Conventional physicians were threatened by homeopathy and its success, arguing that such diluted remedies were useless and that the practitioners were delusional. But as Mark Twain remarked, "Homeopathy forced the old school doctor to stir around and learn something of a natural nature about his business."

Thomson's Herbal Cure

Samuel Thomson (1769-1843) was the first alternative practitioner to reach large-scale popularity—he became so popular, in fact, that some called him the "American Hippocrates." Thomson's well-intentioned reliance on herbal cures stemmed from his mother's death and his wife's near-death at the hands of heroic doctors. Said Thomson of physicians:

> There can be no good reason why all the medical works are kept in a dead language, except it be to deceive and keep the world ignorant of their doings, that they may the better impose upon the credulity of the people, for it was to be written in our own language every body would understand it, and judge for themselves.

Thomson vowed to treat his family himself, and soon extended his services to others as well. Thomson relied heavily on herbs to clean out and restore the body—treatments that were less harmful than heroic medicine, but still mostly useless. Believing that illness stemmed from excessive cold in the body, Thomson treated most everything with hot baths or a vegetable-based remedy that caused sweating. At one point, the Mormon Church declared it their official medicine. Thomson's disgust for conventional physicians is further emphasized with the following verse:

> When sicke, we for the doctor send;
> He says, there is no chance to live,
> Unless I deadly poison give
> When this is done, the sick grow worse,
> Which takes the money from their purse;
> He says, "I've great regard for you,"
> But money is the most in view.

After a visit to Philadelphia, Thomson said that Rush "destroyed more lives than [have] ever been killed by powder and ball in this country in the same time."

Thomson designed a franchise-type system in which his followers had to buy a patent to gain access to his cures. In 1840, Thomson sold more than 100,000 patents. The patent cost about $20 (approximately $350 in today's money), and gave the user a copy of Thomson's book and the right to make and use his remedies. But that wasn't all. Buyers then needed to purchase the herbs from Thomson.

Despite all these rules, Thomson had no way of enforcing them, and his medical wisdom was certainly shared without purchase. Unfortunately for Thomson, he became paranoid of the very people to whom he sold his patents, and disagreed with those who established Thomsonian schools, ultimately leading to the demise of his paying customers.

Curative Waters

Water therapy was also popular and considered a practical cure. An Austrian farmer, Vincent Preissnitz, proclaimed the miracle powers of water in 1829. Preissnitz insisted that water cured his own broken ribs. Water therapy was more of a lifestyle choice than a reaction to disease, and, as with other alternative therapies, its evangelists also recommended healthy living, including bathing, diet, and exercise. (This during a time when it was typical to only bathe once or twice a year.) It came in three different forms: as a bath; by direct application of water onto the affected area; or via consumption or injection. Application sometime meant that patients were wrapped in a freezing cold sheet, wrapped in wool blankets, and left outside for anywhere from twenty-five minutes to several hours, initially shivering and then sweating it out. After this frozen cocoon stage, patients were plunged in cold water and then vigorously dried. Sometimes the showers were so cold that icicles formed! Adherents, whether sick or healthy, were prescribed a minimum of ten to twelve glasses of water a day (today, it is generally agreed that one should drink eight glasses of water a day).

Two American physicians, Joel Shew and Russell Thatcher Trall, spread hydrotherapy stateside. Though water therapists encouraged followers to treat themselves, water-therapy institutes opened across Europe and America. In 1843, the first American hydrotherapy institute opened. Hydrotherapy spas provided a relaxing, exclusive place in the countryside where patients stayed one to three months. (So not so doable for the poor.) After Mark Twain stayed in a European institute, he said, "If I hadn't had a disease I would have borrowed one just to have a pretext for going on."

Ultimately, the popularity of water therapy waned, as fads tend to do. The demise of the hydrotherapy spa was practically guaranteed with the invention of indoor pluming—hot and cold water flowing out of one's home tap meant a special and expensive trip for a curative bath was unnecessary.

Franz Anton Mesmer's Animal Magnetism

The questionable beliefs and work of Franz Anton Mesmer (1734–1815) made it to American shores around the 1830s. The Vienna-trained physician theorized that everyone had an invisible "animal magnetism" that could be manipulated externally, sometimes with magnets or magnetized water, silverware, plates, sheets, and clothing, or with laying of hands or trances. Supposedly, only a small percentage of people could directly influence this "animal magnetism." He claimed that an interrupted flow or blockage of the magnetism caused diseases. (Some liken this to Chinese medicine's *qi*, a flow of vital force along channels in the body.)

Adding to his mystique, Mesmer set the mood with lighting and music and sometimes put his patients into a trance, as in *mesmerized* them. Followers included Wolfgang Amadeus Mozart and Marie Antoinette. (His popularity with Marie Antoinette sparked an investigation by her husband, French King Louis XVI.) Despite the Parisian Royal Commission finding Mesmerism fraudulent (not Mesmer's first brush with scandal), his ideas and practices continued to spread. Like Thomson, Mesmer himself suffered from paranoia, and had a tendency to make enemies of his allies, which ultimately led to his declining popularity.

Charles Poyen—the self-proclaimed "Professor of Animal Magnetism"—then took up the Mesmerism mantle in America, writing an 1837 report, supposedly using respectable sources, proving the legitimacy of animal magnetism. The professor hypnotized audience members, entertaining more than anything. Case in point: Barnum's American Museum included Mesmerism demonstrations. Unlike other irregular practices, Mesmerism never established a real hold in America, but certainly provided an interesting sideshow for a while.

Quacks

Homeopathy, herbal cures, water therapy, and Mesmerism were to varying degrees intended sincerely, but that's not to say that there weren't any outright frauds. In America, traveling medicine shows and bogus medical patents arrived right along with the colonists. Patent medicine might have required a trademark, which had more to do with branding than anything, but there was no regulation whatsoever, and a cure didn't have to be proven to have this stamp of authenticity. In 1849, Mrs. Charlotte Winslow of Maine marketed her "Mrs. Winslow's Soothing Syrup"—a concoction created for children to help them through teething–that contained morphine and alcohol.

"Vital Sparks," a patent medicine that claimed to enhance male virility, was essentially rock candy rolled in powdered aloe. Coca-Cola emerged on the scene in the late nineteenth century as patent medicine created by a morphine addict, Colonel John Pemberton, who sought to create a substitute for his addiction in a unique, French-inspired mixture of cocaine and alcohol. The original Coke supposedly cured everything from headaches to anxiety and indigestion. In 1905, cocaine was eliminated from the soft drink.

The rise of alternative therapies and patent medicine reflected the public's growing concern with the so-called experts' lack of education and professionalism. The prices didn't help either. Members of exclusive, local medical societies ineffectively tried to regulate medicine through their state legislatures. These were essentially attempts to discredit alternative medical practitioners. Extending those efforts to the national level, physicians formed the American Medical Association (AMA) in an attempt to officially legitimize and codify the profession. (One can't help but wonder how one legitimizes treatments that

ADVERTISEMENT FOR MRS. WINSLOW'S, COURTESY OF THE NATIONAL LIBRARY OF MEDICINE

Eat Your Vegetables

Humans throughout the ages have been obsessed with poop and a happy, functioning colon. A humorist once said, "I have finally come to the conclusion that a good reliable set of bowels is worth more to a man than any quantity of wisdom." One of the grossest specimens is a colon from a patient that held more than forty pounds of poop! The colon belonged to a man who, at eighteen months, began to suffer from a disease that halted his colon's full development, preventing waste removal and a brief lifetime of constant constipation. For almost ten years, the young man, only known by the initials of J.W., exhibited himself as "Balloon Man" or "Wind Bag" in a traveling freak show. While on exhibit, it's reported that J.W. liked to pound himself on the stomach and allowed visitors to do so as well, making a drum-like sound. In 1892, at the age of 29, J.W. died in a restaurant's water closet (aka bathroom). At his autopsy, his abdomen's circumference, as measured at the belly button, was 7 feet 2 ½ inches—J.W. was 5 feet, 7 ½ inches tall.

After death, J.W.'s nine-foot colon was part of a sideshow act. Physician Henry F. Formad likened its size to that of a cow.

Today, a chronic megacolon is treated with diet, enemas, and suppositories for regular bowel movement, laxatives, and in some cases, surgery. It is, in other words, not that big of a problem at all.

have no scientific basis?) Professionalism was the main aim, identifying those that violated the code of ethics. The AMA first met in Philadelphia in 1847. Unfortunately, it would take several decades for the AMA to have any real effect amidst the squabbling and chaos of heroic medical practitioners. It's also said that at its inception, the AMA was very elitist in nature, which did nothing to unify the profession and foster agreement. ✴

Chapter 12

WOMEN IN EARLY AMERICAN MEDICINE (OR THE LACK THEREOF)

So far, in recounting early American medical history we've not mentioned very many women, to say nothing of minorities. This is not a deliberate choice, but a historical reality. Traditionally, Western society viewed women as the fairer sex—delicate, of lesser intelligence, and suited only for motherhood. A magazine essay from *The Royal American Magazine* in 1774 argues against the education of women because:

> It deprives the lady of that sweetness, so peculiar to the gentle soul of the fair, and unfits her for the pleasure of social converse. . . Let them, therefore, be well instructed in the polite branches of literature—Let them mature their taste by reading and conversing—without aspiring to be "doctors in petticoats."

Though short-lived, this particular magazine sought to mimic British high society while advocating for American independence. Much like Europe, American culture at the time discouraged women from pursuing an education and working outside of the home. Women who ventured outside this box were harshly judged. Medicine was no exception in restricting a woman's role: Physicians in both Europe and America were not particularly hospitable to female physicians. In 1867, the Pennsylvania Medical Society declared that a woman couldn't handle the role of physician because of her delicate nerves and physiological limitations, the possibility of neglecting domestic duties, and the outrageous possibility of a female physician examining a male patient.

Accusations of Witchcraft

Colonial America's Salem witch trials during the 1690s were just a fraction of the crimes against women healers. In 1484, Reverends Kramer and Sprenger wrote *The Malleus Maleficarum* or *The Hammer of Witches*, a guide to identifying and prosecuting a witch. This illustrious book was the Catholic Church's go-to text for hunting women healers. The Church suggested that a witch was initiated into her power after having sex with the devil. Once in her power, the witch would spread her evil doings and magic under the guise of healing.

Women healers accused of witchcraft were prosecuted beginning in the late 1400s and early 1500s in Europe, especially Germany and Italy. In some German cities, it's estimated that about six hundred witches were burned each year. In Toulouse, France, four hundred were killed in one day. In 1648, Margaret Jones, a Massachusetts midwife accused of witchcraft, was the first to be executed in colonial America.

Healers and Midwives

After the hysteria subsided, the murder stopped, but the discrimination did not. Despite centuries of women healers treating general maladies and acting as midwives, European universities barred women from attending medical programs. American universities followed suit. But the lower and middle classes, unable to afford more expensive physicians, continued to hire women healers—especially as midwives, to help women give birth. Patty Bartlett Sessions (1795–1892), a Mormon midwife, is said to have delivered 3,997 babies in her lifetime, with very few deaths.

Women healers used herbs for treatments and were sometimes called "grannies," passing down their folk wisdom from generation to generation through recipe books. The first American cook-

Risky Business

Pregnancy and birthing were (and still are) a risky undertaking. Given the medical shortcomings of the day, any physical challenges or complications could lead to very dire results indeed. Although accurate statistics on American pregnancy prior to the nineteenth century are hard to come by, it is estimated that one in one hundred live births resulted in the mother's death. Compare that with today's statistics of 15 maternal deaths per 100,000 live births. Medical Journalist Randi Hunter Epstein explains:

> Before forceps, babies stuck in the birth canal were dragged out by the doctor, often in pieces. Sometimes midwives cracked the skull, killing the newborn but sparing the mother. Sometimes doctors broke the pubic bone, which often killed the mother but spared the baby. Doctors had an entire armamentarium[1] of gruesome gadgets to hook, stab, and rip apart a hard-to-deliver baby. Many of these gadgets had an uncanny resemblance to medieval torture tools.

Any added challenges resulted in certain disaster. Mary Ashberry, a dwarf who lived among prostitutes, was three-foot-six and weighed eighty-six pounds. In 1856, a pregnant Ashberry unsuccessfully tried to deliver a baby. In an attempt to save the mother, doctors crushed her baby's skull in the hopes that despite her unusual pelvis, Ashberry could push out the dead child. Unfortunately, those drastic measures did not work, nor did a cesarean section. Ashberry died three days later from abdominal infection. (It's presumptive to suggest, but one can't help but speculate that with today's modern medical advances, Ashberry and her baby would've survived given the commonality of cesarean deliveries, as well the reduced occurrence of infections.)

---

1. A collection of resources.

book, published in 1742, Eliza Smith's *The Compleat Housewife, or Accomplish'd Gentlewoman's Companion*, contained recipes, as well as more than two hundred home remedies for wounds, aches, pains, and more.

Midwifery and all things gynecological remained under the domain of women healers until the mid-1700s, when the wealthy overcame the idea that male physicians should not view a woman's lady parts. Before this change, in 1522, a Hamburg physician, Dr. Wertt, disguised himself as a woman in order to witness a live birth. When outed, Dr. Wertt was burned at the stake under the watch of other physicians.

Benjamin Rush pronounced that women were better off letting nature take its course rather than using a midwife. (Given Rush's questionable medical approach, this is an incredibly patronizing and insulting statement, which was par for the course given his ego.) This transition of male physicians into a traditionally female position—plus the insistence that women should not practice medicine, given their lack of formal education—reduced their roles significantly. But women were generally barred from medical programs. And many male physicians practicing in America were untrained, yet this didn't deter them. Harvard Medical School students had this to say in a letter to Boston's *Daily Evening Transcript* when Harriet Hunt tried to attend their lectures: "Resolved, that no woman of true delicacy would be willing in the presence of men to listen to the discussion of subjects that necessarily come under consideration of the students of medicine." This was despite the fact that school dean Oliver Wendell Holmes and the faculty accepted the notion of Hunt attending.

Hunt did eventually attain a degree, but she had to go the alternative route, graduating with an M.D. degree in Syracuse as a homeopathic physician. Alternative medicine tended to be more accepting of the education of female students.

Challenging the Male Guard

Hunt was one of several female pioneers on the American medical scene. The first woman to gain entry into the club was Elizabeth Blackwell (1821-1910). After several attempts, Blackwell was accidentally accepted to the Geneva School of Medicine in upstate New York. Embarrassed at the prospect of admitting a woman to their program, but politically beholden to her powerful sponsor, the faculty and dean took the matter to their students. Counting on at least one dissenting vote, the dean requested a unanimous student "Yea" for Blackwell's acceptance. As something of a joke, the students came back with the decision to unanimously accept. But it was no joke to Blackwell, and luckily the dean had to honor the decision, however it was intended.

Some citizens of the town took it upon themselves to deliberately ignore Blackwell for her brazenness, but her two years passed without incident for the most part, and in 1849, Blackwell graduated with an M.D. degree, at the top of her class. Along with her sister and German-born midwife Marie Zakrzewska, Blackwell established the New York Infirmary for Women and Children in 1857, which provided a place for women interested in medicine to gain practical experience. It was still not an easy road, one filled with discrimination and rejection.

Another trailblazer, Mary Putnam Jacobi (1842-1906), earned a medical degree from the prestigious University of Paris. She also held previous degrees from the New York College of Pharmacy and The Female Medical College of Pennsylvania—the latter being the first school to offer education and training to women when it opened its doors to forty female students in 1850. Observing that the second year of coursework was a duplicate of the first year at the Female Medical College of Pennsylvania, Jacobi requested to take the exams early and graduated in only a year. Following her medical training, she taught for almost twenty years at Blackwell's New York Infirmary for Women and Children.

Nurses

In England during the Crimean War (1853-1856), nurse Florence Nightingale provided a role model for women on the other side of the pond. Nightingale said of the conditions of wounded soldiers during this war, "There were no vessels for water or utensils of any kind; no soap, towels, or clothes, no hospital clothes; the men lying in their uniforms, stiff with gore and covered with filth to a degree and of a kind no one could write about; their persons covered with vermin. . . ." Motivated by her horror and frustration, Nightingale invented a mathematical chart to illustrate specific causes of the deaths, in hopes of highlighting the need for improved sanitation and nursing practices. Ultimately, the chart demonstrated to her superiors that procedural changes could decrease the preventable deaths of soldiers. It worked. Nightingale dedicated her life to educating future nurses and was the first woman to be awarded the British Order of Merit.

For the male-dominated medical profession, female nurses were at least easier to accept than female physicians. In the decades that followed, nursing (along with teaching) became one of the few societally acceptable jobs for women. The increasing presence of women in American medicine coincided with a larger push by the suffragists (those advocating for women's right to vote) for female rights overall. But it was still a long struggle, and even in the exceedingly chaotic and unprofessional field of American medicine, acceptance of women as equals is happening at a downright glacial pace. In a 1957 questionnaire surveying US male physicians, some choice quotes include "I'd prefer a third-rate man to a first-rate woman doctor" and "women were created to be wives." And in a 2016 study, male doctors earn approximately $20,000 more per year than their female counterparts. ●

Part Three
ANESTHESIA AND CIVIL WAR MEDICINE

Chapter 13

LET'S SKIP THE KNOCK UPSIDE THE HEAD

No stranger to the female struggle for identity in a patriarchal society, British writer Fanny Burney kept extensive journals. While living in France, Burney experienced breast pain. In 1811, a team of physicians removed her breast in a procedure called a mastectomy. In a journal entry, Burney vividly details her mastectomy—done without the aid of anesthesia—as follows:

> Yet—when the dreadful steel was plunged into the breast—cutting through veins—arteries—flesh— nerves—I needed no injunctions not to restrain my cries. I began a scream that lasted unintermittingly during the whole time of the incision—and I almost marvel that it rings not in my Ears still! so excruciating was the agony. When the wound was made, and the instrument was withdrawn, the pain seemed undiminished, for the air that suddenly rushed into those delicate parts felt like a mass of minute but sharp and forked poniards, that were tearing the edges of the wound—but when again I felt the instrument—describing a curve—cutting against the grain, if I may so say, while the flesh resisted in a manner so forcible as to oppose and tire the hand of the operator, who was forced to change from the right to the left—then, indeed, I thought I must have expired.

Burney did not expire from the pain or the surgery. Her experience joins those of countless patients who endured operations before anesthesia.

American dentists were at the forefront of seeking ways to ease surgical pain. It was in their best interest, since dental patients were often repeat customers. (Tooth decay, the gift that keeps on giving.) Though some (from the ancient Sumerians to Europeans during the Middle Ages) thought "tooth worms" caused rot, the introduction of sugar to the European diet in the sixteenth century created a flourishing dental business. Syphilis also created a need. So in demand were healthy human teeth for dentures in the early 1800s, that some sought a profit by stealing sets from corpses. Frequently, substitute materials were used. George Washington's dentures contained human teeth, as well as fake teeth constructed from gold, ivory, and lead.

Tooth powders, the precursor to today's toothpastes, were typically made of ground animal hooves, cuttlefish, or chalk, and did nothing to delay the inevitability of a painful extraction with barbaric tools. This eighteenth-century advertisement for dentures by a dentist practicing in America is typically horrifying:

> He also cures effectually the most stinking Breaths, by drawing out, and eradicating all decayed Teeth and Stumps, and burning the Gums to the Jaw Bone, without the least Pain or Confinement; and putting in their stead, an entire Set of . . . Teeth, set in a Rose-colour'd Enamel, so nicely fitted to the Jaws, that People of the first Fashion may eat, drink, swear, talk Scandal, quarrel, and shew their Teeth, without the least Indecency, Inconvenience, and Hesitation whatever.

The commonality and inevitability of tooth extraction meant that dentists were highly motivated to make patient visits to be less agonizing. Enter, anesthesia.

Numbing the Pain

Nitrous oxide (aka "laughing gas") and ether were identified as gases with pain-killing properties in the late 1700s and early 1800s. Before anesthesia, ether was used to treat scurvy and other medical ailments. Chloroform was first developed by accident, in the process of trying to mix a cheap pesticide. The gases became popular at parties where the wealthy enjoyed the drugs as a recreational intoxicant. Once on the drugs, partygoers didn't realize they had hurt themselves—a fact which, before long, had an obvious use in surgery. (Party on!) It wasn't until several decades later that their medical benefit was recognized.

William E. Clarke and Dr. Elijah Pope first used ether in a tooth extraction in January 1842. Unfortunately, the two did not understand the significance of their actions themselves and did not receive credit for being the pioneers of anesthesia.

Next up in the anesthesia game was Horace Wells, who saw a friend hurt himself without registering any pain at a nitrous-oxide party. As a true guinea-pig scientist, Wells used the drug to remove his own tooth the next day. (Still quite a bit less daring than Hunter's self-experimentation with syphilis.) Excited by his discovery, Wells connected with a former student, William Morton, to demonstrate the tactic in front of John Collin Warren, the professor of surgery at the Massachusetts General Hospital. Unfortunately, the young patient screamed during surgery, though he later admitted that he'd felt no pain. Apparently, the hysterical screaming was due to a nitrous-oxide side effect that was not realized by the audience, or by Wells. Laughing gas can produce unpredictable outbursts such as screaming, moaning, and groaning. Wells' reputation was forever damaged.

The saga continued with an acquaintance of Morton's, Charles Jackson, who wasn't a physician in training or education. However, Jackson was a nitrous-oxide user. With his very personal expertise, Jackson convinced Morton that sulfuric ether combined with air would be more effective than nitrous oxide. Armed with this instruction, Morton, along with John Collins Warren, administered sulfuric ether to a surgical patient. In mid-October of 1846, Morton employed this new approach twice in a row, successfully numbing both patients. In reaction to the achievement, Warren proclaimed: "Gentlemen, this is no humbug." Because of patents and the desire to secure exclusive naming rights, Morton wanted to keep the experiments a secret. But when Morton demonstrated an amputation using a mixture of vapors, a public announcement followed.

Anesthesia to the Rescue

Following the announcement, anesthesia immediately took off both in America and in Europe. Most American physicians gave anesthesia the stamp of approval, but there were a few vocal skeptics at home and across the pond. Administering anesthesia was not without risks, and since it was still in its experimental stages, some patients were killed as a result of incorrect dosages. William Atkinson, a physician and president of the American Dental Association, had this to say about it:

> I think anesthesia is of the devil, and I cannot give my sanction to any Satanic influence which deprives a man of the capacity to recognize the law! I wish there were no such thing as anesthesia! I do not think men should be prevented from passing through what God intended them to endure.

One might guess from his proclamation that Atkinson never himself experienced the pain of surgery.

But back to the drama. Morton and Jackson engaged in a life-long feud over patents, complete with lawsuits. Morton died of a stroke on the way to file another lawsuit against Jackson, leaving only a legacy of poverty. Jackson went insane, as did Wells, who was jailed for throwing sulfuric acid on a prostitute. Wells committed suicide by inhaling chloroform to numb his own pain and then slicing his femoral artery.

Patients didn't care who was correctly credited for successfully discovering and developing the use of anesthesia. Prior to sedation, patients delayed operations to the point of tumors growing to 50 to 100 pounds—anything to avoid the pain and horror of surgery. Anesthesia allowed for surgeons to expand their technical know-how instead of just working for speed. This medical discovery came just in time, as the country was on the brink of civil war, providing ample opportunity for putting it to good use. ✹

Chapter 14

SAWBONES: PRACTICING ON CIVIL WAR SOLDIERS

During the four years of the American Civil War (1861—1865), experts estimated that "Union and Confederate physicians treated more than a half million soldiers with combat wounds and more than 9 million soldiers with diseases such as diarrhea, measles, smallpox, and typhoid fever." (Most medical records from the Civil War are from the Union side, as the majority of Confederate records were burned.) A Union surgeon explained:

> [Physicians] flocked to the colors [joined their respective armies] almost en masse, not only from motives of patriotism, but also because the [medical] training to be gained in the fast military [effort] was far more comprehensive and valuable than could be gained in any similar civil[ian] institute or walk of life.

Practice makes perfect. Hippocrates said, "He who wishes to be a surgeon should go to war." The Civil War provided such an opportunity. As a Union surgeon wrote to his wife, "I have seen more surgery than I could in 50 years of practice."

The chaotic nature of American medicine at the start of the Civil War meant that completely unqualified men enlisted as physicians.

Dr. Alexander T. Augusta, Trailblazer

Born a free man in Virginia and educated in Canada (because American prejudices meant higher institutions wouldn't admit him), Dr. Alexander T. Augusta (1825-1890) was the first African-American surgeon hired by the Union Army. With President Abraham Lincoln's commission, Augusta treated the "colored regiments." At one point, Augusta was reassigned when white surgeons protested. After the war, Augusta eventually settled in Washington, D.C., where he taught at Howard University, becoming the first African American medical professor. Despite the American Medical Association denying Augusta lifelong acceptance as a physician, Augusta actively encouraged African American medical students. Augusta was eventually buried at Arlington National Cemetery with full military honors.

Career army surgeons despised the physician volunteers who had very little medical experience and didn't understand military protocol. These so-called physicians were not prepared for the enormous bloodshed and horrific battlefield conditions. Plus, given the medical education available at the time, it's doubtful that they had even the most basic skills necessary for the desperate circumstances of war. That said, female nurses such as Clara Barton (founder of the American Red Cross) managed to thrive despite overwhelming prejudices and a medical environment rife with politics and bitterness. Medical historian Ian Rutkow summarized that, "American medicine could not have been more contentious at the time of the Civil War."

Abundant Amputations

More American soldiers died in the Civil War than all other wars combined between the Revolutionary War and the Vietnam War. Advances in military technology made matters worse. Inexperienced physicians were especially ill-equipped to treat soldiers gunned down with bullets that shattered upon impact. (This new bullet was called the minié ball, consisting of a softer lead. Its name originates from the inventor, Claude-Étienne Minié, but there was nothing "mini" about it. Its sheer destructiveness led to an overwhelming

CIVIL WAR AMPUTATION WITH ANESTHESIA, COURTESY OF THE NATIONAL LIBRARY OF MEDICINE

number of desperate amputations: three out of every four surgeries resulted in loss of a limb.) The numbing effects of anesthesia, opium, and morphine could only do so much—and they came at a cost, as they were highly addictive as well.

Amputations were often done on a filthy battlefield littered with bodies, where surgeons went from soldier to soldier with the same saw, removing limb after limb in hopes of saving lives. This earned them the nickname of "sawbones." Especially skilled surgeons could remove a limb in under a minute. "Butchers" were those overeager to reach for the saw. After the disastrous loss for Union troops at the Battle of Fredericksburg, a soldier described in a letter home to his mother that he could see pigs from a nearby farm eating human arms and other discarded body parts.

Hot Stuff

In the Middle Ages, the most common treatment for open war wounds was to seal them with boiling oil or with a red–hot iron in order to stop bleeding. In 1563, French barber-surgeon Amroise Paré revolutionized this process of cauterizing, aka sealing, wounds with turpentine, egg yolk, and cream.

There was even a popular parody on the "to be, or not to be" soliloquy from *Hamlet*:

> To amputate, or not to amputate? That is the question.
> Whether tis nobler in the mind to suffer the unsymme-
>   try of one-armed men, and draw a pension.
> Thereby, shuffling off a part of mortal coil.
> Or, trusting unhinged nature, take arms against a cruel
>   surgeon's knife,
> And, by opposing rusty theories, risk a return to dust in
>   the full shape of man.

Apparently, finding the funny in absolutely grim circumstances wasn't that unusual, and was perhaps a useful coping mechanism. A Union nurse tells this story:

> General Howard's right arm was shattered by a ball, so that it had to be amputated above the elbow. Waving the mutilated arm aloft, he cheered on his men, and was borne from the field. While being carried on a litter, he passed General Kearney, who had lost his left arm...Rising on the litter, he called out gayly, "I want to make a bargain with you, General. Hereafter let's buy our gloves together."

Grave Matter

A military reverend rescued the amputated left arm of Confederate General Thomas J. "Stonewall" Jackson (1824-1863) after Jackson's own troops accidentally shot him during the bloody Battle of Chancellorsville in 1863. After surgeons administered chloroform and sawed off the arm, Jackson's personal chaplain, Reverend Lacy, took it to Jackson's family cemetery and gave it a Christian burial and its own grave. Jackson died from pneumonia shortly after the surgery, but was not reconnected with his arm. Supposedly, Union soldiers dug up the arm in 1864 and reburied it, but in reality, its true location remains unknown. A ceremonial headstone, installed by a fellow officer in 1904, commemorates Jackson's arm.

Medical Maggots

Maggots are typically lumped in with all things bad, but there is a medicinal use for maggots. Confederate physician John Forney Zacharias is reported to be the first American to use maggots on his patients' festering wounds, most likely preventing an untold number of unnecessary amputations:

> During my service. . . I first used maggots to remove the decayed tissue in hospital gangrene and with eminent satisfaction. In a single day they would clean a wound much better than any agents we had at our command. I used them afterwards at various places. I am sure I saved many lives by their use, escaped septicaemia, and had rapid recoveries.[1]

Zacharias's ingenuity benefitted soldiers. There's been a modern resurgence in maggot therapy to clean out dead tissue.

---

1. Septicaemia is blood poisoning or sepsis.

The large number of amputees that resulted from the Civil War led to a flourishing business in prosthetics, or artificial limbs. Undoubtedly, some of these amputations were unnecessary, yet it was less risky for a soldier's health to amputate immediately rather than wait (especially more than forty-eight hours) because of the complete inability to reverse a more serious secondary infection which most surgeons were powerless to combat. Civil War surgeons mistakenly considered excretion of yellowish pus in a wound's first stage as a "laudable pus," and saw it as a sign of healing. ●

Chapter 15

ROOM FOR IMPROVEMENT: CIVIL WAR HOSPITALS AND AMBULANCES

Traditionally, armies did not concern themselves overmuch with the lot of their wounded. A Civil War surgeon wrote to his wife describing post-battle horror:

> My Dear Wife;
>
> Day before yesterday I dressed the wounds of 64 different men—some having two or three each. Yesterday I was at work from daylight till dark—today I am completely exhausted—but shall soon be able to go at it again.
>
> The days after the battle are a thousand times worse than the day of the battle—and the physical pain is not the greatest pain suffered. How awful it is—you have nor can have until you see it any idea of affairs after a battle. The dead appear sickening but they suffer no pain. But the poor wounded mutilated soldiers that yet have life and sensation make a most horrid picture.

I pray God may stop such infernal work—through
perhaps he has sent it upon us for our sins. Great indeed
must have been our sins if such is our punishment.

It was a thankless job in which both physician and soldier suffered
immensely, experiencing their own personal hell. It's depressing to
consider that a direct and fatal hit in battle was the easy way to go
during the Civil War.

Death by Disease

The quiet killers of Civil War soldiers on both sides were infection
and disease; medicine had not yet identified microorganisms as the
source for both. Many soldiers were from the countryside and lacked
immunity to city diseases, making them more susceptible to infection. The filthy conditions surrounding the soldiers made it easier for
diseases to proliferate—and that included everything from the cold to
the flu to STDs like gonorrhea and syphilis. Instead of places of healing, battlefield hospitals were miserable places full of soldiers in agony,
dying from neglect or surgical infection.

Officially formed in 1861 at the start of the Civil War, the
United States Sanitary Commission (USSC) was a move in the right
direction. Run and funded by civilians, the USSC sought to spread
the word about improving the water quality, rations, and hospital cleanliness of Union soldiers. (In 1854, John Snow pinpointed
the source of a London neighborhood's cholera outbreak as filthy,
tainted water.) Volunteers collected supplies for soldiers.

Better Wartime Hospitals

In conjunction with the efforts of the USSC, the surgeon general of the Union Medical Department, William A. Hammond
(1828–1900) greatly improved the state of Union military hospitals.
Hammond directed that, when possible, permanent buildings were
constructed rather than making do with vacated churches, barns,
homes, and schools. Permanent buildings translated into more windows, bigger windows, and more space in general—including more
space between patients—provided increased air circulation. This was
critical because, as before, cross-infection among patients with open,

festering wounds was so common that the term "hospitalism" was used to describe the resulting gangrene.

The enhanced conditions in military hospitals, along with better nutrition for patients, led to vastly improved outcomes: "With more than a million men treated as inpatients and overall mortality rate of less than 10 percent, the [Union] army's general hospitals were regarded as invaluable and necessary public institutions." Hospitalism, be gone. Years after the end of the war, Hammond said "that when the war began medical knowledge was only just approaching the end of the medical Middle Ages."

Through the efforts of Hammond and the USSC, there was finally a basic recognition that improving the dietary and sanitary conditions of soldiers fighting and recovering from wounds could help to save lives. One doctor suggested, "Every Army surgeon

Education Not Titillation

One of Surgeon General Hammond's accomplishments was the founding of Washington, D.C.'s Army Medical Museum in 1862, now called the National Museum of Health and Medicine. Its first curator defended the museum against critics who thought it was in poor taste: "[The museum was founded] not for the collection of curiosities, but for the accumulation of objects and data of lasting scientific significance, which might in the future serve to instruct generations of students, and thus in time be productive of real use." They had no interest in creating a freak show.

The Army Medical Museum indicated Hammond's dedication to scientific principles, and his push to link medicine and clinical study. It was one of his earliest efforts to supplement the education of physicians. During the Civil War, bodies were sent to the museum after an autopsy was performed. In a disturbing (but funny) tale, a soldier became upset at finding his amputated limb at the museum. He demanded its return, only to be told by an official that the limb was to remain there until the soldier's term of service was completed. Considering that the soldier's enlistment was not yet over, it was doubtful that the arm's rightful owner would return.

should make it his religious duty to comprehend and control such diseases and causes of disease as are prone to hover about encampments, and secretly break down the strength of armies." Unfortunately, the notion of creating more sanitary conditions did not transfer to insight into germ theory or sterile surgical procedures.

Effective Ambulances

Ideas enacted by Union Surgeon Jonathan Letterman (1824-1872) also improved the lives of the wounded. Following in his physician father's footsteps, Letterman joined the Army Medical Department as an assistant surgeon in 1849. Letterman recognized that it was of the utmost importance to quickly remove injured soldiers from the battlefield. The first ambulances—covered, horse-drawn wagons—were used during the Napoleonic Wars (1799-1815), and were known as *ambulances volantes* meaning "flying ambulances." (Before Letterman initiated the first Ambulance Corps, wounded soldiers were simply left on the field.) Progress was slowed, however, by the fact that Civil War ambulance drivers were known for heavy drinking and desertion. But given battlefield conditions, one can't really blame them.

Treating the injured was a serious problem. One week after the Second Battle of Bull Run in Virginia, of the sixteen thousand Union soldiers needing treatment, Hammond lamented:

> Up to this date, 600 wounded still remain on the battlefield, in consequence of an insufficiency of ambulances and the want of a proper system of regulating their removal. Many have died of starvation; many more will die in consequence of exhaustion, and all have endured torments which might have been avoided.

As if combat were not horrific enough, imagine laying on the battlefield, in agony from an untreated bullet wound, and starving to death.

Henry Bowditch, a professor of medicine at Harvard, became one of the biggest advocates for an organized ambulance corps. In 1862, Bowditch's son was shot in the abdomen, left in the field for two days, and then died of thirst when the ambulance driver refused to bring him water.

Under the Union Army's Letterman Plan, designated stretcher-bearers transported the injured away from the fighting to field stations. Once at the field stations, patients' injuries were categorized into three groups: soldiers who could still walk with minor afflictions, soldiers in need of surgery to ensure survival, and those with mortal wounds who were expected to die. For the last category, drugging the soldiers with opium for pain relief in their dying minutes was the only course of action. Almost a year after Hammond's distress at the chaos of treating soldiers at the Second Battle of Bull Run, the Letterman Plan was instituted at the Battle of Gettysburg, July 1863. Within six hours after the three-day battle ended, 14,193 wounded Union soldiers were treated. Gone were the days of a week-long clean-up that led to unnecessary pain, suffering, and death.

Hammond Disgraced

Despite the fact that Hammond was responsible for many improvements, he was not immune to controversy—and he'd made one very big enemy. His foe was Secretary of War Edwin M. Stanton. Against Stanton's advice, President Lincoln appointed Hammond as Surgeon General. This annoyed Stanton to no end. Stanton's opportunity for revenge presented itself when Hammond outlawed calomel, the mercury compound used for purging. Believing that calomel was harmful, Hammond banned calomel but caused an uproar with petulant American physicians who didn't want to be told what to do. Stanton used this as his chance to get rid of Hammond. In 1863, Hammond was sent on a made-up tour of the South and formally charged and found guilty of poor conduct and irregularities in purchasing medical supplies—irregularities that were based on data fabricated by Stanton. After a dishonorable discharge, Hammond eventually succeeded in clearing his name, only to again face ruin when he made some questionable business decisions that included an employee of his sanitarium, who may or may have not embezzled funds from merchants with his knowledge. ●

Part Four
THE DEATH OF HEROIC MEDICINE

Chapter 16
LISTEN TO LISTER

American physicians who rebelled against Hammond's removal of heroic medicine's supposedly curative calomel from army supplies had no idea what was coming. At the end of the American Civil War, research was underway in Europe that would bring about germ theory and shake the foundation of heroic medicine.

Under the usual conditions of nineteenth-century medicine, a compound fracture (in which a broken bone punctured the skin) almost always resulted in amputation—with the attendant possibility of death from infection. But James Greenlees was a lucky boy when British surgeon Joseph Lister (1827—1912) used his revolutionary antiseptic methods to set Greenlees's shattered shinbone. As Lister explained in his write-up:

> CASE 1.—James G—, aged eleven years, was admitted to the Glasgow Royal Infirmary on August 12, 1865, with compound fracture of the left leg, caused by the wheel of an empty cart passing a little over the limb a little below its middle. The wound, which was about an inch and a half long, and three-quarters of an inch broad, was close to, but not exactly over, the line of fracture of the tibia. A probe, however, could be passed beneath the integument [skin] over the seat of fracture and for some inches beyond it. Very little blood had been extravasated [leaked] into the tissue.

Lister directed his house surgeon to treat and set Greenlees's broken shinbone with cloth soaked in an acid that sterilized the wound and literally killed any chance of infected, rotting flesh. About six weeks after his accident, thanks to Lister, Greenlees was completely healed. This surgery was the beginning of the realization that pus was not only bad, but also preventable.

Identifying Germs

It is said that Louis Pasteur's work on germ theory heavily influenced Lister's conclusion that infected wounds negatively impacted surgery. While studying spoiled wine, beer, and milk, Pasteur demonstrated that microorganisms in the air caused fermentation. Boiling these liquids killed the bacteria, as did the application of filtration or chemical solutions. Lister applied Pasteur's use of chemicals to eliminate bacteria to infected wounds. One medical historian, David Wootton, suggests that Lister downplayed the originality of his germ theory, piggybacking on Pasteur's work in order to gain peer acceptance.

Lister was not the first to advocate for sterilization, but he was the first to specifically address sterilization in terms of wound infection. Lister rejected the long-held belief that pus-filled wound was healthy or good. The solution (pun intended) was carbolic acid, which acted as an antiseptic, killing germs. Carbolic acid is now

Dirty Mouth

Listerine mouthwash was named in honor of Joseph Lister and was originally used as surgical antiseptic. Created in 1879, dentists began to use it as an oral health care product six years later. At one time, it was also sold as a cure for a sexually transmitted diseases, and also used as a floor cleaner. In the 1920s, marketers brilliantly took advantage of consumers by creating a first-time worry about halitosis, aka bad breath. In a scant seven years, Listerine's profits rose from low six figures to $8 million plus. Advertising, once again, preys on the public's insecurities, all in the name of profit.

called phenol. Carbolic acid was used to sterilize the operating room and wounds, before and after surgery (though Lister continued to perform surgery in an apron stiff with dried blood). Also revolutionary was Lister's use of sterile sutures to sew wounds shut.

Unfortunately for other patients at the time, Lister's findings and theory on germs as the cause of infections were not published until 1867 in the medical journal, *The Lancet*. In part, this was due to Lister's admirable and novel efforts to verify the effectiveness of a surgical antiseptic through case studies before making any claims.

Publication was crucial in order for a new medical theory to gain attention and legitimacy. In fact, Cotton Mather, who was responsible for Boston's smallpox vaccination in 1721, identified "tiny animals that were the cause of disease," an idea not picked up until the late nineteenth century. Mather's findings weren't published until the twentieth century, long after his death. In 1683, almost fifty years earlier than Mather, a Dutch microbiologist used his homemade microscope to identify microbes as "little living animalcules" in dental plaque. And in 36 BCE, a Roman scholar warned of "minute creatures" living in swamps that produced diseases. Just how many lives would have been saved if the medical field had connected germs with diseases centuries earlier than it actually did?

Skeptical American Surgeons and Physicians

In 1876, Lister gave a talk in Philadelphia to almost five hundred doctors about the surgical magnitude of infection-free wounds. Lister said of his American counterparts, "American physicians are renowned throughout the world for their inventive genius, and boldness and skill in execution." Despite his praise, Lister received a skeptical reception. Some American surgeons embraced the use of antiseptic in certain aspects of surgery, but most were not believers. Said an American physician, "Little, if any faith, is placed by any enlightened or experienced surgeon on this side of the Atlantic in the so-called carbolic acid treatment of Professor Lister. . . ." Those who did support Lister's theory did so half-heartedly: a clean scalpel would do no good if the surgeon held the instrument in his teeth during the procedure. This was not the place to cut corners. A clean (antiseptic) wound, plus sterile (aseptic) hands and instruments, were key to an infection-free operation. And Lister had the stats to back up his claims: from 1864 to 1866, out of thirty-five operations, Lister's death rate was 45.7 percent. After consistent use of carbolic acid, from 1867 to 1870, out of forty cases, his death rate reduced to 15 percent.

It's theorized that the slow adoption of antiseptic by American surgeons was due to four things: overall confusion, laziness (it was going to take a lot of work to follow Lister's rigorous principles), ineptitude (mistakes made in early applications), and a stubborn reluctance from physicians, who refused to believe in something that they couldn't see. Because of surgical carelessness, initially there wasn't much in the way of significant proof that sterilization via the Lister method was more successful. It wasn't until 1879 in Boston that the first antiseptic surgery in America was performed, and not until the 1890s that the full use of Listerism was applied to American surgery. Ultimately, the sloppiness of American surgeons killed an American president. ●

Chapter 17

KILLING PRESIDENT GARFIELD

No stranger to voicing his opinion, Mark Twain in 1900 summarized the pathetic state of American medicine:

> The doctor's insane system has not only been permitted to continue its follies for ages, but has been protected by the State and made a close monopoly...an infamous thing, a crime against a free-man's proper right to choose his own assassin or his own method of defending his body against disease and death.

And this was Twain's observation after Lister's antiseptic surgical procedures were adopted in America. There is no higher profile example of the utter failure of the system than the death of President James Garfield. On July 2, 1881, Charles Guiteau shot Garfield at a Washington train station. Guiteau was a frustrated would-be politician who felt Garfield had personally snubbed him (despite the fact that the two had never actually met). Garfield was shot in the arm and the back. The arm wound was superficial, but the bullet through the back was thought to have lodged in Garfield's abdomen (in fact, the autopsy revealed that the bullet was near Garfield's spine). The first doctor on the scene gave Garfield alcohol and ammonia to induce purging, and that was just the beginning of many deadly missteps. This event was the catalyst for the American public rejecting the utter nonsense of heroic medicine.

An Ailing President

Dr. D. W. Bliss—a former Civil War surgeon and one of Garfield's childhood friends—was the primary physician on the case. Bliss's initial examination included sticking a metal probe into the wound to search for the bullet. (In Lister's previously mentioned 1876 Philadelphia lecture, he specifically addressed the importance of not touching a bullet wound and trajectory with unclean fingers and instruments!) The dirty probe became stuck amongst the fragments of Garfield's shattered eleventh rib and had to be wrenched free. (Gross, and ouch!) Once freed, Bliss stuck his filthy finger into the wound to continue his unsuccessful search for the bullet. With this failure, physicians moved Garfield back to the White House for treatment.

At the White House, physicians rushed to Bliss's aid. Physician after physician stuck their dirty fingers and instruments into the wound. Concerned that the bullet had hit a major organ, physicians decided not to perform surgery. Even Alexander Graham Bell's newly invented metal detector failed to locate the bullet, as the metal coils in Garfield's mattress led it astray.

The public was enthralled with daily updates of the President's condition. Citizens suggested treatments. And the public grew frustrated when Garfield's health steadily declined.

Infection set in and Garfield's condition worsened. In early September, he was transported to the New Jersey seaside where it was thought that cooler temperatures would help. A special section of railroad track was built for the transfer. With our modern medical knowledge it's not surprising that the cooler temperatures did nothing to improve Garfield's health. On September 19, 1881, after months of fighting for his life, Garfield died—in large part due to sepsis, his body's reaction to the infection. Under the direction of Bliss, in the eighty days that doctors treated Garfield, he lost eighty pounds and his three-inch wound expanded to twenty inches with all the poking and prodding by the physicians. An autopsy indicated that the bullet did pierce a vertebra, but missed all organs and was lodged near his spine.

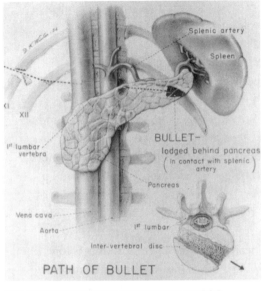

PATH OF BULLET

PATH OF BULLET THAT WOUNDED PRESIDENT GARFIELD,
COURTESY OF WIKICOMMONS

With Garfield's death, Guiteau was charged with murder. His lawyer's defense? Insanity. At one point, Guiteau explained that God made him do it: "The responsibility lies on the Deity, and not on me, and that, in law, is insanity." Ironically, Guiteau also blamed the doctors for killing Garfield: "Nothing can be more absurd, because General Garfield died from malpractice." Rejecting his lawyer's proof that he was legally insane, the jury quickly determined Guiteau's guilt and he was hanged on June 30, 1882. Yet there is certainly truth in Guiteau's claim that medical malpractice caused Garfield's death.

Bliss had the gall to bill Congress $25,000 for Garfield's treatment (estimated to be over $575,000 in today's money), but was awarded only $6,500. Bliss refused this money on principal. In observing the case, doctors who disagreed with Bliss's tactic and remedies remarked, ". . . ignorance is Bliss." The previously mentioned William Hammond asserted in an 1881 article for the *North American Review* that although Garfield's bullet wound was not mortal and the science of surgery was more than equipped to address the damages, Garfield's physicians categorically failed him and caused his death. The American public took note and demanded more of its medicine, wholeheartedly dismissing bleed, blister, puke, and purge. ●

Conclusion

SCIENCE AND MEDICINE FINALLY MEET

In an 1882 editorial in the *Cincinnati Medical Advance*, the editor, T. P. Wilson, M. D. opined:

> . . . we may not look upon the death of our beloved President as wholly in vain. The blunders of the diagnosis, the blunders of the prognosis, the blunders of the treatment, and the blunders of the post-mortem, which so marked and disfigured this world renowned case, will not soon be forgotten; nor should they be forgotten, lest others, however great or humble, should be sacrificed in like manner?

Wilson went so far as to question whether a homeopathic physician could have done better.

After Garfield's death, American medical practice finally began to catch up with medical science. In the 1890s, American physicians and surgeons linked the importance of laboratory work and research to medical schooling. Instead of a backward place dependent on the antiquated medical theories of the Greeks, American medicine transformed into a leader in both education and treatment. Johns Hopkins School of Medicine opened in 1893 and set the new paradigm for a rigorous medical education. America's medical schools improved the quality of their curriculum with grades, graduation requirements, and

Love and Innovation go Hand-in-Hand

William Stewart Halsted, one of the first physicians hired by Johns Hopkins School of Medicine, helped spread Listerism and aseptic surgery with the invention of rubber gloves manufactured by Goodyear Tire and Rubber Company. Halsted was motivated by love: one of his nurses, whom he later married, was allergic to the carbolic acid used to sterilize surgery.

longer terms; many went from two-year programs to three or four. Payment alone no longer secured the title of physician.

Both in Europe and America, medical technology continued to improve and become more readily available. Medical specialization solidified. A year after Garfield's death, in 1882, a physician discovered the bacterial cause of tuberculosis, linking specific microbes to a specific disease. In 1895, X-rays were invented, allowing physicians and surgeons an unprecedented glimpse into the human body. The use of microscopes became widespread in American medical schools during the 1890s, providing previously ignored physical evidence of germs. Sterilization methods were improved, along with the introduction of caps, gowns, and gloves in the operating room.

The combination of anesthesia and sterile surgical procedures revolutionized surgery in America, leading to fewer deaths on the operating table. Bayer's aspirin arrived on the market in 1899. Bloodletting as the medical go-to mostly went out of fashion beginning in the 1920s and is now only sparingly applied in rare cases having to do with iron levels and red blood cell counts in blood. And only small levels of blood are withdrawn, certainly not to the point of passing out like patients of the past.

The use of statistics to record and analyze medical data was another significant step forward. Medical records of treatments and mortality gave doctors insights into the effectiveness of treatments. Medical trials in which a control group of patients does not receive the treatment or medicine that is being tested became standard. This allowed the researchers to distinguish between effective treatments versus the placebo effect. This is today what is referred to as "Evidence Based Medicine." This is a far cry from Rush's insistence that his conclusions were universal because he said so.

Benjamin Rush's overzealous prescriptions to bleed, blister, puke, and purge have been finally laid to rest. Although America's medical Middle Ages are no more, some things haven't changed: mistakes happen, sometimes at the cost of patients' lives. Prejudices meant that a group of African American men with syphilis were unethically denied the antibiotic penicillin all in the name of medical study under the Tuskegee Study of Untreated Syphilis in the Negro Male (1932-1972). Removing part of a mental patient's brain—specifically connections to the prefrontal cortex in the frontal lobe—in a procedure called a lobotomy was all the rage in psychiatry. Neurologist Walter Freeman performed the first American surgery in 1936. The procedure permanently damaged a patient's personality and intellect and was abandoned in the mid-1950s with the advent of anti-psychotic medications. Infections are still a major concern; statistics from 2012 estimate that of the 750,000 people in the United States who experience an infection of some sort, approximately half of them die. A 2016 study by researchers at Johns Hopkins University suggests that the third-leading cause of death in America should be medical errors that range from misdiagnosis to surgical mistakes to prescribing the wrong medicine or the wrong amount. The study estimated that approximately 250,000 patients die each year due to errors, which are not adequately recorded on death certificates, hiding the reality from the American public. Medical practice has vastly improved over the past century, and truly become a science, but, in this and many other ways, history continues to repeat itself. ✸

Bibliography

Anderson, Julie, Emma Shackleton, Emm Barnes, and Antony Gormley. *The Art of Medicine: Over 2,000 Years of Images and Imagination.* Chicago: University of Chicago, 2011.

Asma, Stephen T. *Stuffed Animals and Pickled Heads: The Culture of Natural History Museums.* New York: Oxford University Press, Inc., 2001.

Atherton, David J. "Joseph Towne: Wax Modeler Extraordinary." *Journal of the American Academy of Dermatology* vol. 3, no. 3 (September 1980), pp. 311-316.

Baker, J. A., C. J. Yeo, and P. J. Maxwell IV. "Thomas Dent Mütter: The Humble Narrative of a Surgeon, Teacher, and Curious Collector." *The American Surgeon* vol. 77, no. 5 (2011), pp. 662–664.

Cathcart, H. Robert. "Under Colonial and British Rule." *Philadelphia: A Medical Panorama of 200 Years 1776-1976* (Philadelphia: Philadelphia County Medical Society, 1976), pp. 54–59.

Cristol, David S. "The Early Physicians of Philadelphia." *Philadelphia: A Medical Panorama of 200 Years 1776-1976* (Philadelphia: Philadelphia County Medical Society, 1976), pp. 15-21.

Dobson, Mary. *The Story of Medicine: From Bloodletting to Biotechnology.* New York: Quercus, 2013.

"DR. HAMMOND'S MATRON." *New York Times* (1857-1922): 1. Aug 26 1889. ProQuest. Web access, 7/4/2016.

Ehrenreich, Barbara, and Deirdre English. *Witches, Midwives, and Nurses: A History of Women Healers.* Old Westbury, NY: The Feminist Press at CUNY, 2010.

Fitzharris, Lindsey. "The Battle of the Tooth Worm." *Chirurgeon's Apprentice.* Web. 1/6/2014. Web access, 6/28/2016.

Fitzharris, Lindsey. "Piss Prophets & The Wheel of Urine." *Chirurgeon's Apprentice.* Web. 12/6/2013. Web access, 12/6/2013.

Fleming, Candace, and Ray Fenwick. *The Great and Only Barnum: The Tremendous, Stupendous Life of Showman P.T. Barnum.* New York: Schwartz & Wade, 2009.

Herdon, James H., M.D. "Ignorance is Bliss." *The Harvard Orthopaedic Journal* 15 (December 2013), pp. 74-77. Web access, 5/21/2016.

Hippocrates, translated by Elias Marks, M.D. *The Aphorisms of Hippocrates.* New York: Collins, 1817. *Internet Archive.* Web. 8/10/2010. URL: https://archive.org/details/aphorismsofhippo00hipp. Web access, 6/09/2015.

Jones, Robert Erwin. "Revolutionary Benjamin Rush: Model for the American Physician." *Philadelphia: A Medical Panorama of 200 Years 1776-1976* (Philadelphia: Philadelphia County Medical Society, 1976), pp. 11-14.

Kane, Jason. "The 9 Deadly Diseases That Plagued George Washington." *PBS.* PBS, 7/4/2011. Web access, 12/6/2013.

Kent, Deborah. *Snake Pits, Talking Cures & Magic Bullets: A History of Mental Illness.* Brookfield, CT: Twenty-First Century, 2003.

Leonard, Pat. "William Hammond and the End of the Medical Middle Ages." *Opinionator.* The New York Times, 4/27/2012. Web access, 11/13/2014.

Lindgren, Laura, ed. *Mütter Museum: Historic Medical Photographs.* New York: Blast Books, 2007.

Lovejoy, Bess. "The Gory New York City Riot that Shaped American Medicine." *Smithsonian* (June 17, 2014). Web access, 5/21/2016.

Mauries, Patrick. *Cabinets of Curiosities.* London: Thames & Hudson Ltd., 2002.

Meschter Anders, James. *Philadelphia, World's Medical Centre, by Word and Picture.* Philadelphia: Unknown, 1930.

McClenahan, John L. 'Tales of a "Grand Hospital."' *Philadelphia: A Medical Panorama of 200 Years 1776-1976* (Philadelphia: Philadelphia County Medical Society, 1976), pp. 60-65.

McFarland, Joseph. "Rummaging in the Museum II: The Petrified Lady." *Transactions and Studies of the College of Physicians of Philadelphia* ser. 4, vol. 10 (1942), pp. 138-143.

Murphy, Jim. *The Giant and How He Humbugged America.* New York: Scholastic, 2012.

Nuland, Sherwin B. *Doctors: The History of Scientific Medicine Revealed through Biography.* The Teaching Company, 2005. CD.

Parish, Lawrence Charles, Gretchen Worden, Joseph A. Witkowski, Albrecht Scholz, and Daniel H. Parish. "Wax Models in Dermatology." *Transactions and Studies of the College of Physicians of Philadelphia* ser. 5, vol. 13, no. 1 (1991), pp. 29–74.

Pepper, O. H. Perry. "Benjamin Rush's Theories on Blood Letting After 150 Years." *Transactions and Studies of the College of Physicians of Philadelphia* ser. 3, vol. 14 (1946), pp. 121-126.

Roy, Porter. *Blood and Guts. A Short History of Medicine.* First American Edition. New York: W W Norton, 2003.

Sappol, Michael. "A Cabinet of Curiosities." *Common-place: Morbid Curiosity.* The Interactive Journal of Early American Life, Jan. 2004. Web access, 11/5/2013.

Wade Ellen N. "The History and Growth of the Mütter Museum." *Transactions and Studies of the College of Physicians of Philadelphia* ser. 4, vol. 14 (1946), pp. 24-28.

Warner, John Harley and James M. Edmonson. *Dissection: Photographs of a Rite of Passage in American Medicine 1800-1920. First Edition.* New York: Blast Books, 2009.

Whitfield J. Bell Jr. "Medical Students and Their Examiners in Eighteenth Century America." *Transactions and Studies of the College of Physicians of Philadelphia* ser. 4, vol. 21 (1953), pp. 14-24.

Williams, William Henry. "*The Pennsylvania Hospital, 1751-1801: An Internal Examination of Anglo-America's First Hospital.*" PhD thesis. University of Delaware, 1971.

Wisswaesser, Catherine. "Roots and Ramifications of Medicinal Herbs in 18th-Century America." *Transactions and Studies of the College of Physicians of Philadelphia* ser. 4, vol. 44 (1977), pp. 194-199.

References

CHAPTER 1

Rutkow, Ira M. *Bleeding Blue and Gray: Civil War Surgery and the Evolution of American Medicine* (New York: Random House, 2005).

Rutkow, Ira M. *Seeking the Cure: A History of Medicine in America* (First Edition. New York: Scribner, 2010).

CHAPTER 2

Percy, George. "*Jamestown: 1607, the First Months.*" Observations Gathered out of a Discourse of the Plantation of the Southern Colony in Virginia by the English, 1606. (London: 1608). Web access, 4/8/2016.

Dobson, Mary. *The Story of Medicine: From Bloodletting to Biotechnology* (New York: Quercus, 2013).

Steele, Volney. *Bleed, Blister, and Purge: A History of Medicine on the American Frontier* (Missoula, Montana: Mountain Press Pub, 2005).

Rothstein, William G. *American Physicians in the Nineteenth Century: From Sects to Science.* Softshell Books Edition. The John Hopkins University Press, 1992.

Coffin, Margaret M. *Death in Early America: The History and Folklore of Customs and Superstitions of Early Medicine, Funerals, Burials, and Mourning* (Nashville: Thomas Nelson Inc., Publishers, 1976).

Rutkow, Ira M. *American Surgery: An Illustrated History* (Philadelphia: Lippincott-Raven Publishers, 1998).

Pickover, Clifford A. *The Medical Book: From Witch Doctors to Robot Surgeons: 250 Milestones in the History of Medicine* (New York: Sterling Pub., 2012).

Crosby, Alfred W. *The Columbian Exchange: Biological and Cultural Consequences of 1492* (30th Anniversary Ed. Westport, CT: Praeger, 2003. Contributions in American Studies No. 2).

Willard, Fred L., Victor G. Aeby, and Tracey Carpenter-Aeby. "Sassafras in the New World and the Syphilis Exchange." *Journal of Instructional Psychology* vol. 41 (2014), 5. Web access, 4/5/2016.

CHAPTER 3

Ruschenberger, W. S. W. "An Account of the Institution of the College of Physicians of Philadelphia: Notice of Dr. Abraham Chovet." *Transactions and Studies of the College of Physicians of Philadelphia* ser. 3, vol. 9 (1887), lxxviii. Web access, 12/5/2014.

Norris, George W. *The Early History of Medicine in Philadelphia* (Philadelphia: Collins Printing House, 1886), 93. Web access, 9/14/2015.

Worden, Gretchen. *The Mütter Museum: Of the College of Physicians of Philadelphia.* First Edition (New York: Blast Books, 2002).

CHAPTER 4

Franklin, Benjamin. *Some Account of the Pennsylvania Hospital from Its First Rise to the Beginning of the Fifth Month, Called May, 1754* (Philadelphia: Printed at the Office of the United States' Gazette, 1817), 4. Web access, 11/12/2014.

Graham, Kristen A. *A History of the Pennsylvania Hospital* (Charleston, SC: The History Press, 2008).

Norris, George W. *The Early History of Medicine in Philadelphia* (Philadelphia: Collins Printing House, 1886), 93. Web access, 9/14/2015.

Wilbur, C. Keith. "*Revolutionary Medicine 1700-1800*" (Philadelphia: Chelsea House Publishers, 1980).

Worden, Gretchen. *The Mütter Museum: Of the College of Physicians of Philadelphia.* First Edition (New York: Blast Books, 2002).

CHAPTER 5

Graham, Kristen A. *A History of the Pennsylvania Hospital* (Charleston, SC: The History Press, 2008).

Morton, Thomas G and Frank Woodbury. *The History of the Pennsylvania Hospital, 1751-1895* (Philadelphia: Times Printing House, 1895), ix. Web access, 1/19/2016.

Packard, Francis R. *The History of Medicine in the United States a Collection of Facts and Documents Relating to the History of Medical Science in This Country, from the Earliest English Colonization to the Year 1800, with a Supplemental Chapter on the Discovery of Anesthesia* (Philadelphia: J.B. Lippincott, 1901), 342. Web access, 11/13/2014.

Packard, Elizabeth Parsons Ware. *The Prisoner's Hidden Life, or, Insane Asylums Unveiled; As Demonstrated by the Report of the Investigating Committee of the Legislature of Illinois, Together with Mrs. Packard's Coadjutors' Testimony* (Chicago: The Author, A. B. Case, printer, 1868), 14. Web access, 6/6/2016.

CHAPTER 6

Radbill, S. X. "Medicine in 1776: Colonial and Revolutionary Medicine in Philadelphia." *Transactions and Studies of the College of Physicians of Philadelphia* ser. 2, vol. 44 (1976).

Bell, Whitfield J. *John Morgan, Continental Doctor* (Philadelphia: U of Pennsylvania, 1965).

Bauer, Edward Louis. *Doctors Made in America* (Philadelphia: Lippincott, 1963), 4. Web access, 6/28/2016.

McClellan, George. *Principles and Practices of Surgery* (Philadelphia: Grigg, Elliot, and Co., 1848), 78. Web access, 6/28/2016.

Mütter Exhibits Manager, Evi Numen. Personal Interview. November 2011.

Aptowicz, Cristin O'Keefe. *Dr. Mütter's Marvels* (New York: Gotham Books, 2014).

Gibbon, John H. "Thomas Dent Mütter: Professor of Surgery, Jefferson Medical College, 1841-1856." *Transactions and Studies of the College of Physicians of Philadelphia* ser. 3, vol. 47 (1976).

CHAPTER 7

Coffin, Margaret M. *Death in Early America: The History and Folklore of Customs and Superstitions of Early Medicine, Funerals, Burials, and Mourning* (Nashville: Thomas Nelson Inc., Publishers, 1976).

Duffy, John. *From Humors to Medical Science: A History of American Medicine* (Second Edition. Urbana, IL: University of Illinois Press, 1993).

Zacks, Richard. *An Underground Education: The Unauthorized and Outrageous Supplement to Everything You Thought You Knew about Art, Sex, Business, Crime, Science, Medicine, and Other Fields of Human Knowledge* (New York: Anchor Books, 1997).

Dobson, Mary. *The Story of Medicine: From Bloodletting to Biotechnology* (New York: Quercus, 2013).

Jones, Nora L. *"The Mütter Museum: The Body as Spectacle."* PhD thesis (Ann Arbor, MI: University of Michigan, 2002).

Wade Ellen N. "A Curator's Story of the Mütter Museum and College Collections" *Transactions and Studies of the College of Physicians of Philadelphia* ser. 4, vol. 42 (1974).

CHAPTER 8

Horden, Peregrine, and Elisabeth Hsu. "Humours and the Hippocratic Corpus." *The Body in Balance: Humoral Medicines in Practice* (New York: Berghahn Books, 2013), 30. Web access, 6/12/15.

Parker, Steve. *Kill or Cure: An Illustrated History of Medicine* (London: Dorling Kindersley Limited, 2013).

Dobson, Mary. *The Story of Medicine: From Bloodletting to Biotechnology* (New York: Quercus, 2013).

Nuland, Sherwin B. *Doctors: The History of Scientific Medicine Revealed Through Biography.* Chantilly, VA: Teaching Co, 2005. Lecture 3. Sound recording.

Davis, Audrey and Toby Appel. *The Project Gutenenberg EBook of Bloodletting Instruments in the National Museum of History and Technology.* Web. 7/7/2010. URL: http://www.gutenberg.org/files/33102/33102-h/33102-h.htm#f19.1. Web access, 5/5/2015.

Rothstein, William G. *American Physicians in the Nineteenth Century: From Sects to Science.* Softshell Books Edition. The John Hopkins University Press, 1992.

Zacks, Richard. *An Underground Education: The Unauthorized and Outrageous Supplement to Everything You Thought You Knew about Art, Sex, Business, Crime, Science, Medicine, and Other Fields of Human Knowledge* (New York: Anchor Books, 1997).

Rutkow, Ira M. *Bleeding Blue and Gray: Civil War Surgery and the Evolution of American Medicine* (New York: Random House, 2005).

Rutkow, Ira M. *Seeking the Cure: A History of Medicine in America* (First Edition. New York: Scribner, 2010).

CHAPTER 9

Drinker, Cecil Kent, and Elizabeth Sandwith Drinker. *Not So Long Ago: A Chronicle of Medicine and Doctors in Colonial Philadelphia*. (New York: Oxford UP, 1937), 41. Web access, 12/16/2014.

Coffin, Margaret M. *Death in Early America: The History and Folklore of Customs and Superstitions of Early Medicine, Funerals, Burials, and Mourning* (Nashville: Thomas Nelson Inc., Publishers, 1976).

Duffy, John. *From Humors to Medical Science: A History of American Medicine* (Second Edition. Urbana, IL: University of Illinois Press, 1993).

Sheldon, George F. "Rush and Physick: An Important Medical Friendship." *Transactions and Studies of the College of Physicians of Philadelphia* ser. 4, vol. 29 (1961).

Shryock, Harrison. "Benjamin Rush from the Perspective of the Twentieth Century" *Transactions and Studies of the College of Physicians of Philadelphia* ser. 4, vol. 14 (1946).

Janik, Erica. *Marketplace of the Marvelous: The Strange Origins of Modern Medicine* (Boston: Beacon Press, 2014).

Zacks, Richard. *An Underground Education: The Unauthorized and Outrageous Supplement to Everything You Thought You Knew about Art, Sex, Business, Crime, Science, Medicine, and Other Fields of Human Knowledge* (New York: Anchor Books, 1997).

Steele, Volney. *Bleed, Blister, and Purge: A History of Medicine on the American Frontier* (Missoula, Montana: Mountain Press Pub, 2005).

CHAPTER 10

Gawande, Atul. "Two Hundred Years of Surgery." *The New England Journal of Medicine* 366 (2012), 1718. Web access, 3/24/15.

Graham, Kristen A. *A History of the Pennsylvania Hospital* (Charleston, SC: The History Press, 2008).

Duffy, John. *From Humors to Medical Science: A History of American Medicine* (Second Edition. Urbana, IL: University of Illinois Press, 1993).

Dobson, Mary. *The Story of Medicine: From Bloodletting to Biotechnology* (New York: Quercus, 2013).

Graham, Kristen A. *A History of the Pennsylvania Hospital* (Charleston, SC: The History Press, 2008).

Worden, Gretchen. *The Mütter Museum: Of the College of Physicians of Philadelphia*. First Edition (New York: Blast Books, 2002).

Wade Ellen N. "A Curator's Story of the Mütter Museum and College Collections" *Transactions and Studies of the College of Physicians of Philadelphia* ser. 4, vol. 42 (1974).

CHAPTER 11

Roy, Porter. *Blood and Guts. A Short History of Medicine*. First American Edition. New York: W W Norton, 2003.

King, Lester S. *The Medical World of the Eighteenth Century* (Chicago: The University of Chicago Press, 1958).

Janik, Erica. *Marketplace of the Marvelous: The Strange Origins of Modern Medicine* (Boston: Beacon Press, 2014). Rothstein

Rothstein, William G. *American Physicians in the Nineteenth Century: From Sects to Science*. Softshell Books Edition. The John Hopkins University Press, 1992.

Rutkow, Ira M. *Seeking the Cure: A History of Medicine in America* (First Edition. New York: Scribner, 2010).

Steele, Volney. *Bleed, Blister, and Purge: A History of Medicine on the American Frontier* (Missoula, Montana: Mountain Press Pub, 2005).

Formad, Henry F. "A Case of the Giant Growth of the Colon Causing Coprostasis or Habitual Constipation." *Transactions of the College of Physicians of Philadelphia* ser. 3 vol., 14 (1892).

CHAPTER 12

Leander. "On the Education of the Fairer Sex." *The Royal American Magazine* (1774).

Aptowicz, Cristin O'Keefe. *Dr. Mütter's Marvels* (New York: Gotham Books, 2014).

Dary, David. *Frontier Medicine: From the Atlantic to the Pacific, 1492-1941* (New York: Alfred A. Knopf, 2008).

Coffin, Margaret M. *Death in Early America: The History and Folklore of Customs and Superstitions of Early Medicine, Funerals, Burials, and Mourning* (Nashville: Thomas Nelson Inc., Publishers, 1976).

Helmuth, Laura. The Disturbing, Shameful History of Childhood Deaths." *Slate*. Web. 9/10/2013. Web access, 7/4/2016.

Lyons, Albert S. "Medical History—Women in Medicine." *Health Guidance*. Web. 12/17/2012. URL: http://www.healthguidance.org/entry/6355/1/Medical-History—Women-in-Medicine.html. Web access, 11/14/2014.

Parker, Steve. *Kill or Cure: An Illustrated History of Medicine* (London: Dorling Kindersley Limited, 2013).

Pickover, Clifford A. *The Medical Book: From Witch Doctors to Robot Surgeons: 250 Milestones in the History of Medicine* (New York: Sterling Pub., 2012).

Oaklander, Mandy. "Women Doctors are Paid $20,000 Less than Male Doctors." *Time*. Web. 7/11/2016. Web access, 7/11/2016.

CHAPTER 13

Kaplan, Michael. "THE NEW JACKSONIAN BLOG." *Breast Cancer in 1811: Fanny Burney's Account of Her Mastectomy*. N.p., Web. 12/2/2010. URL: http://newjacksonianblog.blogspot.com/2010/12/breast-cancer-in-1811-fanny-burneys.html. Web access, 9/9/2014.

Duffy, John. *From Humors to Medical Science: A History of American Medicine* (Second Edition. Urbana, IL: University of Illinois Press, 1993).

Dobson, Mary. *The Story of Medicine: From Bloodletting to Biotechnology* (New York: Quercus, 2013).

Rutkow, Ira M. *Bleeding Blue and Gray: Civil War Surgery and the Evolution of American Medicine* (New York: Random House, 2005).

Rutkow, Ira M. *American Surgery: An Illustrated History* (Philadelphia: Lippincott-Raven Publishers, 1998).

CHAPTER 14

Uschan, Michael V. *A Civil War Doctor* (Detroit: Lucent, 2005).

Roy, Porter. *Blood and Guts. A Short History of Medicine*. First American Edition. New York: W W Norton, 2003.

Rutkow, Ira M. *Bleeding Blue and Gray: Civil War Surgery and the Evolution of American Medicine* (New York: Random House, 2005).

Rutkow, Ira M. *American Surgery: An Illustrated History* (Philadelphia: Lippincott-Raven Publishers, 1998).

Root-Bernstein, Robert S, and Michèle Root-Bernstein. *Honey, Mud, Maggots, and Other Medical Marvels: The Science Behind Folk Remedies and Old Wives' Tales* (Boston: Houghton Mifflin, 1997).

CHAPTER 15

Rutkow, Ira M. *Bleeding Blue and Gray: Civil War Surgery and the Evolution of American Medicine* (New York: Random House, 2005).

"*Antietam National Battlefield: Letters and Diaries of Soldiers and Civilians*." (n.d.): n. pag. National Parks Service. URL: http://www.nps.gov/anti/learn/education/upload/Letters%20and%20Diaries%20of%20Soldiers%20and%20Civilians.pdf. Web access, 4/7/2015.

Uschan, Michael V. *A Civil War Doctor* (Detroit: Lucent, 2005).

CHAPTER 16

Lister, Joseph. "On a New Method of Treating Compound Fracture, Abscess, Etc. with Observations of the Conditions of Suppuration, Part I." *The Lancet* (March 16, 1867), 327. Web access 9/14/2015.

Wootton, David. *Bad Medicine: Doctors Doing Harm since Hippocrates* (Oxford: Oxford UP, 2006).

Duffy, John. *From Humors to Medical Science: A History of American Medicine* (Second Edition. Urbana, IL: University of Illinois Press, 1993).

Pickover, Clifford A. *The Medical Book: From Witch Doctors to Robot Surgeons: 250 Milestones in the History of Medicine* (New York: Sterling Pub., 2012).

Rutkow, Ira M. *Seeking the Cure: A History of Medicine in America* (First Edition. New York: Scribner, 2010).

Rothstein, William G. *American Physicians in the Nineteenth Century: From Sects to Science*. Softshell Books Edition. The John Hopkins University Press, 1992.

Trueman, C. N. "Joseph Lister." *The History Learning Site*. Web. 3/17/2015. URL: http://www.historylearningsite.co.uk/joseph_lister.htm. Web access, 5/8/2015.

CHAPTER 17

Janik, Erica. *Marketplace of the Marvelous: The Strange Origins of Modern Medicine* (Boston: Beacon Press, 2014).

Herr, Harry W. "Ignorance is Bliss: The Listerian Revolution and Education of American Physicians." *The Journal of Urology* 177 (2007), 458. Web access, 5/27/2016.

The Death Of President Garfield, 1881. 2012. URL: http://www.eyewitnesstohistory.com/gar.htm.

"*American Eras: Development of the Industrial United States, 1878-1899*." Ed. by V. Tompkins et al. Vol. 8. American Eras. Detroit: Gale Research, 1997. Chap. Garfield and Guiteau.

Rutkow, Ira M. *Seeking the Cure: A History of Medicine in America* (First Edition. New York: Scribner, 2010).

Wilson, T. P. "1882 Editorial." *Cincinnati Medical Advance* vol. 12, no. 1 (January 1882), 21. Web access, 5/27/2016.

"Sepsis Fact Sheet." *National Institute of General Medical Sciences*. National Institute of General Medical Sciences. Web. Aug. 2014. URL: https://www.nigms.nih.gov/education/pages/factsheet_sePSIs.aspx. Web access, 5/27/2016.

Allen, Marshall, and Olga Pierce. "Medical Errors Are No. 3 Cause Of U.S Deaths, Researchers Say." *NPR*. NPR. Web. 5/3/2016. URL: http://www.npr.org/sections/health-shots/2016/05/03/476636183/death-certificates-undercount-toll-of-medical-errors. Web access, 5/27/2016.

Index

Acknowledgments

It may be a cliché, but writing *Bleed, Blister, Puke, and Purge* has been a journey, one involving an extensive network of cheerleaders and supporters. In both the book and these acknowledgments, all historical inaccuracies and inadvertent omissions are mine.

Eternal gratitude to my husband, Sameer, whose forthright manuscript feedback made me cry a few times. Thanks for your insight, humor, patience, academic library card, and kiddo patrol. To Tristin and Jayde, apologies for all of the gruesome surgical volumes lying around the house—hopefully it will be worth it when you someday read this book. Otherwise, therapy is on me.

Kudos to friends-turned-readers: Mike, Janet, Linda, Liz, Lesley, and Tony. All provided invaluable input, persevering despite the awkward, early drafts. To Laurie for her generous mentoring—SCBWI WWA is lucky to have you!

Appreciation goes to Michelle Witte, my agent who believed in a truly odd topic and sold it like a rock star. Not only that, but Michelle cleaned up my dangling modifiers, a herculean task. Gold star for her patience.

I am so fortunate that *Bleed, Blister, Puke, and Purge* landed with Zest Books. My editor, Dan, asked all the right questions and whipped the narrative into shape. Adam, you are a graphics wizard, I couldn't have hoped for a better look. Thanks to Emma, a publicist extraordinaire, who also agrees that riding horses is the best.

Gratitude to the Mütter Museum's staff, especially former exhibits curator Evi Numen, and Pennsylvania Hospital's archivist Stacey Peeples. Both were generous with their time, providing access to their collections, as well as feedback on the manuscript. Also, shout-out to the tireless, unnamed workers who scanned and uploaded copyright-free medical histories—thanks to you, the world is literally at one's fingertips.

Lastly, to the kick-ass teens and library staff I've had the good fortune of working with and learning from: this book is for you.

About the Author

J. Marin Younker worked as a public librarian for thirteen years, book-talking in the schools, leading book groups, talking to teens, and managing teen collections. She earned a degree in history from Western Washington University, and now lives in the Seattle area with her family and animal menagerie.